Contents

About your BTEC Level 2 Award in Door Supervision and BTEC Level 2 Award in Security Guarding

BTEC Level 2 Award in Door Supervision and BTEC Level 2 Award in Security Guarding are qualifications that are designed to provide specialist work-related qualifications. They give the learner the knowledge, understanding and skills they need in order to prepare for employment.

BTEC Level 2 Award in Door Supervision is designed for people who want to work as door supervisors and require a licence to practise. The qualification is endorsed by the Security Industry Authority (SIA), and learners who complete it successfully can apply to the SIA for a licence.

For this qualification you must complete the following mandatory units:

- Unit 1 Working in the private security industry
- Unit 2DS Working as a door supervisor
- Unit 3 Conflict management for the private security industry
- Unit 4 Physical intervention skills for the private security industry

BTEC Level 2 Award in Security Guarding is designed for people who require a licence to practise in order to work as a contracted security officer. The qualification is endorsed by the Security Industry Authority (SIA), and learners who have completed it successfully can apply to the SIA for a licence.

For this qualification you must complete the following mandatory units:

- Unit 1 Working in the private security industry
- Unit 2SO Working as a security officer
- Unit 3 Conflict management for the private security industry

How to use this book

This book is designed to help you through your BTEC Level 2 Award in Door Supervision and BTEC Level 2 Award in Security Guarding. The book contains many features that will help you use your skills and knowledge in work-related situations and assist you in getting the most from your course.

Introduction

The introduction on the first page of each unit gives you a snapshot of what is covered in the unit – and what you should be aiming for by the time you finish it!

1 Working in the private security industry

This unit is designed for people who want to work in the private security industry and who require an SIA licence to practise. It covers the most common areas of working in the private security industry:

* Door supervision
* Security guarding
* CCTV operations
* Vehicle immobilisations
* Cash and valuables in transit.

In this unit you will find out about the key requirements across the security sector, including how the security sector operates, the employment opportunities within it, the key legislation that applies to the industry and how you can keep yourself and others safe in the workplace. You will also learn about effective communication and customer care.

Learning outcomes

After completing this unit you should:

1. know the purpose and main features of the private security industry
2. understand the legislation that is relevant to people working within the private security industry
3. know how to maintain health and safety in the workplace
4. know how to apply the principles of fire safety
5. know how to deal with non-fire-related workplace emergencies
6. understand the principles of effective communication and customer care in the private security industry.

Case studies

Case studies provide a snapshot of real workplace issues and situations and include thought-provoking questions and discussion points.

Case study: Anna, Hospital security

We deal with all kinds of things here, from regulating the parking to providing physical security for the premises and monitoring the CCTV used around the hospital site. Hospitals don't close so we operate on a 24-hour rota. Friday and Saturday nights are our busiest time as you get people with alcohol-related injuries and a lot of the time the people who come with them are drunk as well. It's a recipe for trouble. We try to keep the hospital staff as safe as possible by dealing with trouble early. There is no point getting aggressive or angry with someone who is drunk and injured – it doesn't help anyone – so we deal with it really calmly and firmly. Most of the time we can head off trouble, but where we can't, the police in this area are very supportive. Security in a hospital can be really difficult to get right: you've got to remember that some of the people you are dealing with will be ill or upset and you have to tread carefully. It's not as straightforward as working somewhere like a shopping centre.

Over to you

1. How might working in a hospital be different from working in a shopping centre?
2. What are the essential qualities Anna might look for in her team members?
3. Why is a good relationship with the police needed?

Key terms

Technical words and phrases are picked out in blue throughout the book to make them easy to spot, and a definition of each key term appears in the margin. All the key terms and their definitions are collected in the glossary at the back of the book.

Key term

Absconding – leaving, often to avoid prosecution

Activities

The questions in the activities will give you a broader grasp of the industry, and develop and deepen your skills.

Activity: Other sectors

Using the internet, research the four security roles listed and find out what the jobs involve and whether you need an SIA licence to do them.

Workspace

The Workspace page at the end of each unit contains a real workplace case study and questions to help you think about how the skills and knowledge you develop during your course can help you in your career.

WorkSpace
Cortez Marshall
Senior security officer in a local government office

The city centre offices I work in deal with all kinds of council issues, from social housing repairs to benefits claims. It can be a very busy and noisy environment and we were finding we were having lots of security incidents at busy times such as Saturday morning. We reviewed the way the space was set up and spoke with customers who were having difficulties and it became clear that the security we had set up to protect staff was actually having a detrimental impact. The safety glass in front of the council workers was impairing how well they could hear the members of the public and was leading to misunderstandings and frustrations. We had created a single waiting area for everyone for ease of surveillance, but the noise level made effective communication impossible. We decided to redesign the space to make communication easier and faster by removing the security glass, structuring different waiting areas for different issues and ensuring security staff were seen as a source of support to the public not as a threat. We have recorded 76% less security incidents per month as a result of the changes.

Over to you

1. What were the key issues with effective communication in this situation?
2. Why would not being able to communicate effectively cause difficulties for the security team?
3. Can you think of any premises you know where the design could be a problem for security?
4. If you were Cortez what would you have done about the situation?

Just checking

At the end of each unit there is a set of quick questions to see how much you can remember about what you have just learned.

Just checking

1. What are the main purposes of the security industry?
2. What are the main functions of the SIA?
3. What are the key differences between civil and criminal law?
4. List the eight principles of the Data Protection Act.
5. What is the name of the key piece of legislation governing health and safety in the workplace?
6. List the typical hazards that can cause trips, slips and falls.
7. What injuries are and are not reportable under RIDDOR?
8. What are the three components of a fire?
9. Describe the five common fire classifications.
10. How would you define an emergency?
11. In the case of a bomb threat, what questions would you ask the caller?
12. What are common barriers to communication?
13. Why is effective communication important?
14. What types of customer are you likely to come into contact with?
15. What are the six golden rules when dealing with customer issues?

BTEC Specialist

edexcel
advancing learning, changing lives

DOOR SUPERVISION & SECURITY GUARDING

LEVEL 2 Award

Debra Gray | Andy Element | Alannah Burke

A PEARSON COMPANY

Published by Pearson Education Limited, a company incorporated in England and Wales, having its registered office at Edinburgh Gate, Harlow, Essex, CM20 2JE. Registered company number: 872828

www.pearsonschoolsandfe.co.uk

Text © Pearson Education Limited 2011
Edited by Sally Clifford
Designed by Lorraine Iinglis
Typeset by Phoenix Photosetting, Chatham, Kent
Original illustrations © Pearson Education Limited 2011
Illustrated by Phoenix Photosetting
Cover design by Visual Philosophy, created by eMC Design
Cover photo/illustration © **Pearson Education Ltd/Roddy Paine**

The rights of Debra Gray, Andy Element and Alannah Burke to be identified as authors of this work have been asserted by them in accordance with the Copyright, Designs and Patents Act 1988.

First published 2011

12 11 10 09
10 9 8 7 6 5 4 3 2 1

British Library Cataloguing in Publication Data
A catalogue record for this book is available from the British Library.

ISBN 978 1 446900 10 9

Printed in the UK by Scotprint

There are links to relevant websites in this book. In order to ensure that the links are up to date and that the links work we have made the links available at www.pearsonhotlinks.co.uk

Acknowledgements
The author and publisher would like to thank Victoria Arms, Old Marston, for providing the location for the photoshoot, and Gary Burford and Stephan Hamilton for stepping in to offer their assistance.

The publisher and authors would like to thank the following for their kind permission to reproduce their photographs:
Alamy Images: Chris Pancewicz 45, Corbis Flirt 116, Denkou Images 109, Jon Parker Lee 77, Jupiter Images 15, Stephen Barnes / Medical 60, The Illustrated London News Picture Library. Ingram Publishing. 2; **Pearson Education Ltd:** David Sanderson 18, Gareth Boden 138, MindStudio 159, Naki Kouyioumtzis 3, Richard Smith 1, 11, 24, 79, Roddy Paine 5, 37, 39, 40, 42, 46, 49, 58, 61, 62, 67, 69, 72, 106, 111, 129, 133, 139, 142, 144, 146, 149, 150, 153, 155, **Shutterstock.com:** AlexandreNunes 108, ANATOL 94, BelleMedia 124, c. 80, Creation 19/4, Cycreation 19/6, Dana Smith 65, Derter 19/1, Ebtikar 27t, Eoghan McNally 10, Evstigneev Alexander 34, Helder Almeida 76, hkannn 29, Kaspri 19/2, 19/3, Kenneth Man 8, Leah-Anne Thompson 16, Luminis 82, mmaxer 102, Nicholas Piccillo 143, Olivier Le Queinec 99, Owen1978 19/5, R.Ashrafov 36, Raulin 84, Scott Bowlin, siart 70, STILLFX 88, Vichie81 91, Yobidaba 19/7, Yuri Arcurs 158
All other images © Pearson Education

The publisher and authors would like to thank the following for their kind permission to use their materials:
p.11 Eight principles of the data protection act adapted from The Data Protection Act 1998 in accordance with the terms of the Open Government License for public sector information (for information, see http://www.nationalarchives.gov.uk/doc/open-government-licence/open-government-licence.htm)
p.43, quote from Criminal Law Act 1967 reproduced in accordance with the terms of the Open Government License for public sector information
p.69, quote from Licensing Act 1964 reproduced in accordance with the terms of the Open Government License for public sector information
p.70, quotes from Licensing Act 1964 reproduced in accordance with the terms of the Open Government License for public sector information
p.112 quote reproduced with kind permission of ASNED (the Association of Sustainable Night-time Economy Development)
p.144 proof of age poster reproduced with kind permission of www.answers.uk.co

Every effort has been made to contact copyright holders of material reproduced in this book.
Any omissions will be rectified in subsequent printings if notice is given to the publishers.

Disclaimer
This material has been published on behalf of Edexcel and offers high-quality support for the delivery of Edexcel qualifications. This does not mean that the material is essential to achieve any Edexcel qualification, nor does it mean that it is the only suitable material available to support any Edexcel qualification. Edexcel material will not be used verbatim in setting any Edexcel examination or assessment. Any resource lists produced by Edexcel shall include this and other appropriate resources.

Copies of official specifications for all Edexcel qualifications may be found on the Edexcel website: www.edexcel.com

1 Working in the private security industry

This unit is designed for people who want to work in the private security industry and who require an SIA licence to practise. It covers the most common areas of working in the private security industry:

- Door supervision
- Security guarding
- CCTV operations
- Vehicle immobilisations
- Cash and valuables in transit.

In this unit you will find out about the key requirements across the security sector, including how the security sector operates, the employment opportunities within it, the key legislation that applies to the industry and how you can keep yourself and others safe in the workplace. You will also learn about effective communication and customer care.

Learning outcomes

After completing this unit you should:

1. know the purpose and main features of the private security industry
2. understand the legislation that is relevant to people working within the private security industry
3. know how to maintain health and safety in the workplace
4. know how to apply the principles of fire safety
5. know how to deal with non-fire-related workplace emergencies
6. understand the principles of effective communication and customer care in the private security industry.

What do you already know?

As you have chosen to complete this short course it is likely that you have decided you want to make a career for yourself in the private security sector, but how much do you already know about the industry?

Working individually or in pairs, list as many locations as you can where you might find private security employees working. You may be surprised by how widespread and specialised they are.

Once you have your list, rank the areas where you could work in order of preference. This will help you focus on the content of this unit and apply it to where you would most like to work. Share your list and preferences with your assessor or the rest of your group.

1. Know the purpose and main features of the private security industry

The private security industry in the UK is very large and profitable. The British Security Industry Association (BSIA) estimates that over 75,000 security officers are employed in the UK with an additional 300,000 across other areas of the sector such as consultancy, door supervision, CCTV operation, close protection work and vehicle immobilisation. The sector as a whole has an annual turnover in excess of £4 billion, which is growing year on year. Understanding the purpose and main features of the private security industry is essential if you hope to build your career within it.

1.1 Main purposes of the private security industry

The private security industry has existed for hundreds of years and pre-dates the creation of the police service in 1829. Wealthy individuals and businesses have always required protection from those who would seek to do them harm or steal their goods and property. Before the creation of the police service in the UK it was the private security industry who often prevented and investigated crimes, and brought criminals to justice. These individuals were called 'watchmen' or 'thief takers' and were hired by individuals to prevent theft, capture those responsible and return any stolen goods. Close protection work or 'bodyguarding' has an even longer history with historical accounts describing bodyguards employed to protect Egyptian pharaohs and Roman and ancient Chinese emperors.

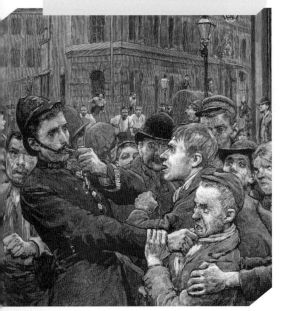

Police work in London in 1895. Things have changed a lot since then.

With the creation of a professional police service in the UK, the role of the private security industry became more specialised. The following (discussed in more detail below) are the main focuses of the industry today:

- Prevention and detection of crime and unauthorised activities.
- Prevention and reduction of loss, waste and damage.
- Monitoring and responding to safety risks.

Prevention and detection of crime and unauthorised activities

The vast majority of the security industry is highly visible, for example, security guards are uniformed, security signs are large and prominent, and CCTV cameras are placed in visible locations. The reason for this is so that the security measures can act as a deterrent to individuals who might be looking to commit a crime. A criminal may look at these visible measures and be prevented from taking any further action. It is far more cost effective to prevent a crime than to deal with the after-effects of one. In addition, many insurance companies will give significant discounts to companies and individuals who have 24-hour security; for very high-risk venues the discount from the insurance company can actually exceed the total cost of the security. Visible security might also prevent members of the public and company employees engaging in unauthorised activities. The term 'unauthorised activities' is very broad and varied and can cover anything the company does not want employees or the public to do.

Prevention and reduction of loss, waste and damage

Security personnel and equipment at a venue can help monitor and reduce loss of goods from theft. This includes not only external sources of theft such as shoplifting and burglary, but also internal theft by employees. If there is a fire, the presence of security personnel reduces the average cost of repair and replacement work as the fire can be detected earlier and brought under control more quickly.

Monitoring and responding to safety risks

Security personnel and equipment are often deployed to respond to known safety risks, for example, they may perform access control at building entrances and exits. This includes checking authorisation to enter premises and searching for weapons, drugs or other prohibited material. Security personnel may also be required to respond to minor emergencies and supervise / evacuate at major emergencies until the uniformed public services arrive on the scene.

CCTV cameras are a good preventative measure. Can you think of any others?

Did you know?

Examples of employees engaging in unauthorised activities caught on security CCTV in recent years include:

- urinating in a coffee pot
- having sex on company premises
- selling illegal substances on company premises
- using business equipment for personal gain
- using food that has fallen on the floor to sell to the public
- deliberately throwing packages to break them
- taking a bath in a sink
- sexually harassing female staff.

Key terms

Deterrent – anything that prevents someone from doing something, e.g. a fence, a guard dog, a CCTV camera etc.

Unauthorised activities – actions which a company or individual does not permit on their premises. Unauthorised activities are not always illegal.

Prohibited – banned or not authorised.

1.2 Sector and career opportunities

The private security industry employs over 300,000 people in the UK in a variety of different roles. It is important for you to be familiar with the main sectors so you can make an informed choice about where you want to work.

Licensed sectors in manned guarding

There is a requirement in the UK for security personnel to have a licence to operate, which is awarded by the Security Industry Authority (SIA). The types of work that require a licence are defined in the Private Security Industry Act 2001. Table 1.1 below lists the licensed sectors and a brief description of them.

> ### Key term
>
> Absconding – leaving, often to avoid prosecution

Table 1.1: Licensed sectors

Licensed sector	Description
Cash and valuables in transit	This is where high-risk goods such as money or antiques are moved between venues in specially adapted vehicles. There is a higher risk of theft when goods are on the road than when they are securely locked away in a vault and therefore they need additional security protection. This could also apply to the transport of suspects and prisoners to and from courts and prisons where they are at greater risk of absconding or being helped to escape.
Close protection	This used to be known as 'bodyguarding' and involves protecting an individual who may be at risk of assault or injury. This is not as straightforward as preventing a physical attack taking place; it also includes other work such as carrying out a premises check before a client arrives, calming threatening situations, helping clients get to and from venues safely, and escorting clients nationally or internationally on social and business trips.
Door supervision	Before the private security industry was regulated this type of work was known as 'bouncing'. It involves ensuring the safety and security of employees and customers at a specific venue such as a nightclub, pub or large public event. Door supervision includes a variety of duties such as checking identification, searching for weapons or drugs, checking tickets, dealing with conflict, escorting people from the premises, responding to emergencies and completing reporting paperwork.
Public space surveillance (CCTV)	A CCTV operative normally works in front of a bank of monitors operating on a shift system over a 24-hour period. A single operator could be responsible for fifteen screens each receiving live pictures from over 100 cameras on a rotating basis. Their primary role is to monitor the screens and notify security staff or the police if they see a crime or suspicious activity.
Security guard	Security guards are often thought of as private police officers, although it is important to note that they do not have any more powers than an ordinary member of the public. They do a variety of work including patrols, responding to alarms, controlling access to premises, deterring theft and criminal damage, and resolving conflict.
Immobilisation, restriction and removal of vehicles	This type of work involves the management of vehicles that are not on a public road (e.g. vehicles on private business premises or privately owned land or in private car parks). The work includes restricting the movement of vehicles by clamping, removal of vehicles from the property, charging for the return of vehicles and charging for the removal of clamping.

Table 1.1 (cont.)

Licensed sector	Description
Key holding	Private security personnel are sometimes asked to be key holders for the venues they protect. This is a position of great trust as you will have 24-hour access to premises in case of an alarm call out. A key holder's role involves the following duties: responding to call outs, knowing how to gain access to premises, dealing with the alarm system, contacting the owner and the police, resetting the security systems and locking up the premises.

If you are planning to work in the sectors described above you will have to hold an SIA licence, which is issued in the form of a plastic card and costs £245 for a three-year registration period. Vehicle immobilisers must pay £245 for a one-year licence period.

Other sub–sectors

As well as manned guarding there are other areas of security work that you could choose to go into, such as:

- private investigation
- events security
- electronic security
- fire systems.

Career opportunities in operational roles

Most well-run private security firms have a clear and accountable management structure and you may decide that you want to work as a manager or supervisor within the industry. If so, you still need to carry an SIA licence, but it is more likely to be a non-front line licence, which is issued in the form of a letter that also covers key holding activities.

Career opportunities in support roles

No private security company could run effectively without a great deal of support from the non-operational staff who perform a variety of roles to ensure that security personnel are able to do their jobs effectively. This includes:

- sales staff who ensure there is plenty of work available for operational personnel
- human resources to ensure personnel are paid and trained appropriately
- specially trained security consultants who help businesses and individuals decide on the most appropriate security services for their needs.

Did you know?

Security personnel who work 'in house', i.e., employed by a company directly, are not required to hold an SIA licence.

Activity: Other sectors

Using the internet, research the four security roles listed and find out what the jobs involve and whether you need an SIA licence to do them.

SIA licence is clearly displayed on duty

1.3 Aims of the Private Security Industry Act 2001

Before the creation of the Private Security Industry Act 2001 there was great concern that the security sector, which had significant responsibility for the safety of the public, premises and goods, was unregulated and unmonitored. This meant that anyone could work within the sector and hold a position of trust and responsibility, even if they had criminal convictions or had no training to do the job.

The Private Security Industry Act 2001 addressed some of these concerns by creating a new regulator (the SIA) to ensure all security personnel are trained and suitable for their job. The key aims of the SIA act are summarised in Figure 1.1 below.

Figure 1.1: Key aims of the SIA act

1.4 Main functions of the SIA and other key bodies

The SIA was established in 2003 to act as the regulator for the private security industry. It acts to monitor the private security industry and ensure that companies in the sector are well managed and trustworthy. It also acts to raise standards within the industry in terms of training for staff and compliance with regulations. It has two main roles:

- The compulsory licensing of individuals undertaking specific activities within the private security industry, such as security officers and door supervisors, as described in Table 1.1 on page 4.

- Managing the voluntary Approved Contractor Scheme (ACS), which measures private security suppliers against independently assessed criteria. This ensures the standards used by private security companies are high and that they are trustworthy.

Did you know?

The Security Industry Authority (SIA) can remove a security company from the Approved Contractor Scheme (ACS) if they do not comply with regulatory requirements. This effectively means that it would be harder for them to operate in the sector.

In essence the SIA works with the security industry to ensure its employees are properly trained and qualified. This means that those who buy security services can have confidence in the companies they purchase from. One of the key difficulties is that the ACS is voluntary which means that companies do not have to join it. However if you were in the market for security services would you rather choose a regulated company or an unregulated one? Although it may not be compulsory for security firms to register with ACS, it acts as a hallmark of quality in the industry.

Standard-setting bodies (setting standards in non-licensed roles)

The key standard-setting body for the security industry is Skills for Security. It is a Sector Skills Council (SSC) and it has decided on the national occupational standards needed by the security industry.

Inspectorate bodies for SIA Approved Contractor Scheme

A security company must go through an assessment process to become an approved contractor. The SIA allows carefully regulated organisations to act as inspectors / assessors and inspect the quality of security offered by the companies and decide whether they are fit to be approved contractors.

All approved contractors must be inspected every year to make sure their standards are as high as required. In 2009/10 there were 674 approved contractors who employed a total of 123,000 security operatives. However in the same year 22 companies failed their inspection and had their approved contractor status taken away from them.

1.5 Main qualities required for security industry operatives

Working in the security industry can place you in a position of great trust and responsibility. You will need to demonstrate personal qualities that show you are worthy of the trust your employer and your clients place in you.

Reliability – You must be punctual and always carry out your set duties. A security guard who decides not to do the required amount of patrols or who fails to respond to an alarm may cost a client a great deal of money and damage their employer's reputation.

Integrity – You may have access to thousands of pounds' worth of merchandise or equipment so your honesty and integrity should never be in question. You must always act in the best interests of your employer and their client.

Did you know?

You can find the national occupational standards for the security industry at the Skills for Security website. For a link to the site, please visit www.pearsonhotlinks.co.uk

Did you know?

The current SIA assessing bodies are:
- British Standards Institution
- National Security Inspectorate
- ISOQAR
- Security Systems and Alarm Inspection Board
- Chamber Certification Assessment Services.

Observational skills – Good observational skills are important in most of the job roles in the industry. If you are working as a CCTV operative, you may spend the bulk of your working day looking for anything out of the ordinary in your field of view. Similarly security guards on patrol have to be aware of anything unusual which might indicate problems.

Politeness – It is likely that you will be working with the public a great deal. If you are polite, the public are more likely to listen to you and comply with your requests.

Communication skills – As well as dealing with the public, you are likely to be dealing with the emergency services, premises owners and your own security teams. The ability to communicate well will help you a great deal in these areas of your role.

Being prepared to take responsibility to solve problems – There may be occasions when you are working alone, or at night, or away from immediate help, so you must have the skills and confidence to deal with whatever problems you encounter until help arrives.

Ability to handle sensitive situations – Working in the security industry you will come across a wide variety of situations that may require you to be tactful, diplomatic and sympathetic while carrying out your duties.

Team-working skills – You must be able to show that you are able to work as part of a team, supporting your colleagues while doing a difficult job.

Case study: Anna, Hospital security

We deal with all kinds of things here, from regulating the parking to providing physical security for the premises and monitoring the CCTV used around the hospital site. Hospitals don't close so we operate on a 24-hour rota. Friday and Saturday nights are our busiest time as you get people with alcohol-related injuries and a lot of the time the people who come with them are drunk as well. It's a recipe for trouble. We try to keep the hospital staff as safe as possible by dealing with trouble early. There is no point getting aggressive or angry with someone who is drunk and injured – it doesn't help anyone – so we deal with it really calmly and firmly. Most of the time we can head off trouble, but where we can't, the police in this area are very supportive. Security in a hospital can be really difficult to get right: you've got to remember that some of the people you are dealing with will be ill or upset and you have to tread carefully. It's not as straightforward as working somewhere like a shopping centre.

Over to you

1. How might working in a hospital be different from working in a shopping centre?

2. What are the essential qualities Anna might look for in her team members?

3. Why is a good relationship with the police needed?

2. Understand the legislation that is relevant to people working within the private security industry

In order to be successful in the private security industry you must know about the laws that have an impact on how you can do your job. The next section of this unit looks at some of these laws.

2.1 Civil and criminal law

There are key factors that determine whether a crime falls under civil or criminal law. These factors are outlined in Table 1.2 below.

Table 1.2: Key differences between civil and criminal law

	Civil law	Criminal law
Purpose	Civil law governs the relationship between individuals or businesses. For example, if you have a bad haircut and you decide to sue the barber, this will be a civil law case as it only involves you and the hairdresser, and doesn't involve breaking the law. The courts most likely to deal with civil issues are the small claims court and the county court. The purpose of civil law is to right a wrong.	Criminal law governs the relationship between the individual and the state. For example, if you break a law which has been set by the state then the state has the right to prosecute you. The courts most likely to be involved in this are the Magistrates' court and the Crown Court. The purpose of criminal law is to punish the individual and deter others from doing the same thing.
Who brings the cases	In civil law the case is brought by the individual who feels they have been wronged and the case is written like this: *Smith v. Quick Cutz Barber* Smith is the person who has had the poor haircut and Quick Cutz is the company he alleges is responsible.	In criminal law the case is brought by the state against the individual who has broken the law. It is written like this: *R. v. Hague* R stands for Rex or Regina (King or Queen) and Hague is the person who broke the law.
Remedy	The remedy in civil law is usually financial compensation.	The remedy in criminal law can be a fine, prison sentence or community penalty.
Standard of proof	The standard of proof in civil law is 'the balance of probabilities'. This means the court must weigh up the evidence and decide who is more likely to be right.	The standard of proof in criminal law is 'beyond reasonable doubt'. This means the court must be absolutely certain before making a decision to convict.

Activity: Standard of proof

The standard of proof in civil and criminal cases is different. Why do you think this is? What could be the consequences if criminal courts weren't absolutely sure before they made a conviction? Write down your thoughts.

2.2 Relevance of human rights legislation

Activity: Human rights

Look at the list of human rights. Which ones might impact upon the private security industry the most? Explain your reasons.

Human rights legislation applies to every individual and company operating in the country. The main piece of legislation is The Human Rights Act 1998 which came into force on 2 October 2000 although it is complemented by the Data Protection Act 1998 (see page 11) and the Freedom of Information Act 2000. It is particularly important to the security industry as it covers issues such as privacy.

The Human Rights Act 1998 puts into law the principles agreed in the European Convention on Human Rights. Its aim is to defend the rights and freedoms of the public and promote democracy. One of the key concepts in human rights is that they apply to all people equally, regardless of their gender, ethnicity, sexuality, religion or any other defining characteristic. They should be universally applied to all individuals without prejudice.

The key rights and freedoms which UK citizens have include:

- Right to life
- Freedom from torture and inhumane or degrading treatment
- Right to liberty and security
- Freedom from slavery and forced labour
- Right to a fair trial
- No punishment without law
- Respect for private and family life, home and correspondence
- Freedom of thought, belief and religion
- Freedom of expression
- Freedom of assembly and association
- Right to marry and start a family
- Protection from discrimination in respect of these rights and freedoms
- Right to peaceful enjoyment of your property
- Right to education
- Right to participate in free elections.

Freedom of expression is enshrined in the European Convention on Human Rights

2.3 Data protection principles

There are eight principles in the Data Protection Act which are outlined in Figure 1.2 below.

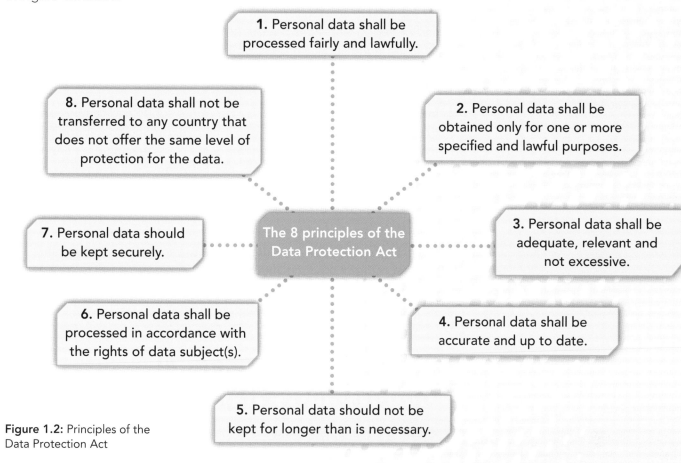

1. Personal data shall be processed fairly and lawfully.

8. Personal data shall not be transferred to any country that does not offer the same level of protection for the data.

2. Personal data shall be obtained only for one or more specified and lawful purposes.

The 8 principles of the Data Protection Act

7. Personal data should be kept securely.

3. Personal data shall be adequate, relevant and not excessive.

6. Personal data shall be processed in accordance with the rights of data subject(s).

4. Personal data shall be accurate and up to date.

5. Personal data should not be kept for longer than is necessary.

Figure 1.2: Principles of the Data Protection Act

2.4 Discrimination in the workplace

Discrimination is a term that means treating a person or a group less favourably based on their personal characteristics or membership of a social group. These characteristics or social groups could include any of the following:

- race
- ethnicity
- gender
- religion
- disability
- sexual orientation
- age.

Discrimination means treating a person or group less favourably based on their personal characteristics or membership of a social group.

Types of discrimination

There are two main types of discrimination:

Direct discrimination – This is the more obvious type of discrimination, for example, if an ethnic minority job candidate with more experience and better qualifications doesn't get an interview while a less well qualified white applicant does, or if a disabled employee is ignored for promotion in favour of less-experienced candidates who are not disabled.

Indirect discrimination – This is often more subtle and can be harder to detect and prove. It involves an employer putting conditions in place that adversely affect one group of people more than another and are not a real requirement of the job role. For example if an employer specified that a candidate must be six feet tall, this would proportionally disadvantage women who are on average shorter than their male counterparts.

It is important to know the difference between these two terms. In general, indirect discrimination is lawful if it can be shown to be a necessary and proportionate way to achieve an aim (such as physical tests to show fitness for a job role), whereas direct discrimination is usually unlawful.

2.5 Areas where equal opportunities legislation applies

Ensuring equal opportunities is in the best interests of the employer as well as the employee. If an employer discriminates against certain groups they may not get the best candidate for the job. There are key areas where equal opportunities legislation applies in the workplace.

Recruitment – Recruitment must be based on the requirements of the job role only. There are very few jobs that require highly specific personal characteristics in order to be done well. The colour of a security officer's skin does not indicate how well they will do the job and the sexual orientation of a CCTV operator does not affect their observational skills. Recruitment should not be influenced by the personal **prejudices** of the employer.

Access to training – All employees must have the same rights to training for the job role they do. Access to training can vary between jobs as the requirements for each role will be different, but an employer should ensure that employees who are doing the same role have equal access to the training they need in order to be effective.

Pay and benefits – Individuals should be paid in accordance with their work and performance. This should be fair and transparent.

Key terms

Prejudice – a negative opinion about another person based on their outward appearance or social group.

Victimisation – the term used when an employer retaliates against an individual who has made a complaint against them (e.g. the employer refuses the employee a reference).

Harassment – any behaviour which is unacceptable to the recipient and creates an atmosphere of intimidation or fear.

Promotion opportunities – Promotion opportunities should be offered to individuals based on their performance and effectiveness rather than their personal characteristics.

Terms and conditions – The terms and conditions for employees ought to be made on the basis of their job role rather than their personal characteristics. The terms and conditions ought to be fair and transparent and applicable to each person doing the same role.

Redundancy – When an employer is in the position of having to make redundancies, the decision who to make redundant needs to be made in accordance with legislation, not in accordance with race, colour or religion. Employers must be fair.

Dismissal – Dismissing an employee is usually a last resort for an employer. However, they need to make sure that where they make a dismissal, it is based on job performance rather than their personal prejudices.

The employer's duty to make reasonable adjustments for disabled people – Every employer must make reasonable adjustments to enable individuals with disabilities to work effectively and productively.

> **Did you know?**
>
> There are some jobs which can be advertised under the Equality Act 2010 as having an occupational requirement for particular characteristics. For example, there are occasions in the field of drama and entertainment when individuals of a specific race or colour may be needed to make a production 'genuine' or realistic. In the field of personal care, a candidate may need to be either a male or a female to protect the privacy and dignity of their patient, and if a church is advertising for the post of a minister it makes sense for them to have a requirement that the candidate must believe in a particular religion.

3. Know how to maintain health and safety in the workplace

Working in the private security industry can be hazardous. An SIA study found that half of security guards had been subject to some form of violence and 94% of door supervisors who had worked in the industry for five years or more had been attacked. Employers and employees have a joint responsibility to take steps to ensure **risk** is controlled and workers and the public are as safe as possible.

> **Key term**
>
> Risk – the chance that someone might be harmed by, or as a result of, a hazard.

3.1 Importance of Health and Safety

Health and safety is very important in the private security industry. The key piece of legislation that governs workplace safety is the Health and Safety at Work Act (1974). The Health and Safety Executive (HSE) produces a health and safety poster that should be displayed prominently in your place of work, which details the responsibilities of the employer and the individual and outlines what to do if you have a health and safety problem.

> **Activity: The Health and Safety Executive**
>
> You can find a link to the HSE website at www.pearsonhotlinks. co.uk. Download the 'Introduction to Health and Safety' booklet which you will find in the guidance section. Read it and make notes on the aspects of health and safety that you may need additional training or guidance on. Speak with your tutor or employer about receiving this additional training.

Key terms

Control measure – a preventative measure put into place to try and make sure that a hazard does not cause a high risk (e.g. a zebra crossing on a busy road, protective boots and a hard hat on a building site, a high-visibility jacket at night).

Hazard – anything that may cause harm, e.g. working at heights, lone working or fire.

Compliance

It is very important that you and your employer comply with legislation, as the consequences of failing to comply can be severe and include prosecution by the HSE and eventual closure of the business. In addition, failure to comply with health and safety legislation can lead to:

- lost productivity. If staff are injured and cannot work, a company will not be operating as efficiently as it could be.

- disruption to the business. If health and safety is not complied with, a business could be closed and lose its customers.

- staff shortages. If staff are ill or injured, it will be difficult to have a full staff rota.

- long-term health effects. Injuries and illnesses can lead to long-term problems for staff, such as acute back pain, which can affect them for the rest of their lives.

3.2 Responsibilities under health and safety legislation

Both employers and employees have responsibilities under health and safety legislation. Table 1.3 below looks at employers's main areas of responsibility, and Table 1.4 includes employees' and self-employed people's main areas of responsibility.

Table 1.3: Employers' main duties under health and safety legislation

Duty	Explanation
Assess and reduce risk	Employers must conduct a risk assessment of your working conditions and situation and implement appropriate control measures. They must also carry insurance which covers employees if they get hurt at work.
Provide first aid facilities	Employers are responsible for providing adequate first aid facilities. These might take the form of a trained first aider and an emergency first aid kit.
Tell staff about hazards	Employees must be told clearly where the hazard is, what the risk is, how it will be controlled and who will be responsible for this. Workers who do not know the risks in a workplace will be less able to protect themselves from illness or injury as a result.
Provide training if required	Employers must provide, free of charge, the health and safety training you need in order to do your job.
Record injuries and accidents	Employers must record and report to the HSE injuries, diseases and dangerous incidents at work.
Provide and maintain necessary equipment	An employer must provide, free of charge, any equipment you need in order to do your job and ensure this equipment is kept in safe working order.
Provide and maintain necessary clothing	An employer must provide you with personal protective equipment (PPE) free of charge.
Provide and maintain necessary warning signs	It is an employer's duty to ensure safety signs are clearly visible and well maintained.

Table 1.4: Employees' and self-employed people's main duties under health and safety legislation

Duty	Explanation
Take responsibility for own health and safety	You must take responsibility by following the training you have received from your employer and using the equipment you are given as it is meant to be used.
Cooperate with employer	Your employer can only protect you if you cooperate with them. All the PPE, safety signs and risk assessments in the world won't help you if you choose to ignore them.
Take reasonable care and not put themselves or public at risk	You must ensure your actions or inaction do not put the safety of yourself, your colleagues or the public at risk.
Report injuries and accidents to employer	You must ensure you report any problems to your employer. Employers can only deal with issues they are aware of.

3.3 Ways of minimising risk to personal safety and security

Developing awareness of risks and hazards

Being aware of your environment and the potential risks and hazards in it is a key part of working in the private security industry. One of the quickest ways to educate yourself on health and safety issues is to take some risk awareness and risk assessment training. You could ask your employer to pay for this or you could pay for it yourself.

Training on specific hazards

A general awareness of risks and hazards is just the starting point for working in the security industry. Security personnel work in a wide variety of settings and must be familiar with any specific hazards that occur in those settings. For example, security personnel working in situations where they need to perform body searches on members of the public may need specific hazard training on needles and sharp objects. Personnel working in airport security may need specific training regarding suspect packages. Door supervisors may need specific training in dealing with physical and verbal abuse.

Did you know?

Employers must also ensure that employees have access to toilets, washing facilities and drinking water.

Activity: Responsibilities

Identify the main responsibilities of employees, employers and the self-employed under health and safety legislation.

Activity: Specific hazards

Consider the following venues that you might be employed in as part of the security industry:
- a nightclub
- a hospital
- a shopping centre
- a steelworks
- a university.

Can you think of any specific hazards you might find in these venues that will require specific training?

Use of personal alarms and mobile phones

Security personnel may work alone or some distance from their nearest source of support. It is therefore important that they are able to raise an alarm or contact supervisors, colleagues or the police if an incident occurs. Many security personnel are issued with radios, alarms and mobile phones by their employers as a risk control measure.

Importance of following safe routines and being systematic

It is important that you protect your health and safety by ensuring you follow set safety routines exactly. They are put in place for your protection. If you choose not to follow them you are compromising your own safety, the safety of others and your employer's business.

Procedures for lone working

Lone workers are those who work by themselves without close or direct supervision, such as security officers on patrol or those acting as the sole security officer at a client's premises at night. Working alone can pose a particular set of risks as immediate help and assistance will not be available in the event of an incident.

It is the employer's duty to consider the issues of lone working and draw up a risk assessment to reduce the risks. Things an employer may consider include:

- Lost productivity – If staff are injured and cannot work a company will not be operating as efficiently as it could be.
- Is there a safe way in and out for one person?
- Is there a risk of violence?
- Are there any chemicals or hazardous substances being used that may pose a risk to the worker?
- Can all the machinery and goods involved in the workplace be handled safely by one person?
- Is more than one person needed to operate essential controls for the safe running of equipment or workplace transport?

Lone workers need to be experienced in their role and understand the risks and control measures in place to protect them. They should be very clear about what they can and cannot do when working alone, and be able to deal with the unexpected. There are several possible control measures which can be put into place to protect lone workers, including:

- regular visits from a mobile supervisor

Security personnel who conduct body searches may need specific hazard training.

- regular contact via radio, phone or e-mail between a lone worker and their base

- automatic alarms that trigger if the lone worker does not send specific signals to a supervisor at specific times

- checks by supervisors to ensure a lone worker has arrived home safely.

The Health and Safety Executive is the government body responsible for making sure health and safety legislation and risk assessments are followed and that businesses and organisations take all reasonable steps to protect people. They recommend five steps to risk assessment:

- **Step 1** – Identify the hazards (e.g. trailing wires, spills, electrical equipment, broken glass, chemicals, lone working, working at height)

- **Step 2** – Decide who might be harmed and how (e.g. yourself, the public, by falling, electric shock, chemical burns, verbal abuse)

- **Step 3** – Evaluate the risks and decide on precautions (e.g. Is it low risk, medium risk or high risk? Precautions could include PPE, safety signs, mopping up spills, removing broken glass, ensuring first aid is present)

- **Step 4** – Record your findings and implement them (e.g. put them on a formal risk assessment)

- **Step 5** – Review your assessment and update if necessary.

Activity: Risk assessment

You are required to patrol a building site at night as a lone worker. How could you make yourself safer using the five steps to risk assessment described above?

3.4 Typical hazards in the workplace

One of the most common hazards found in the workplace is slip / trip hazards. They make up a third of all major injuries; each year over 10,000 workers suffer serious injuries as a result of a slip or a trip.

Did you know?

The cost to employers of slips and trips is £512 million per year in loss of productivity and other costs.

Factors that cause slips and trips

Figure 1.3 on page 18 lists some of the common causes of slips and trips.

Table 1.5 gives some of the key requirements that should be checked in facilities to reduce the likelihood of slips and trips occurring.

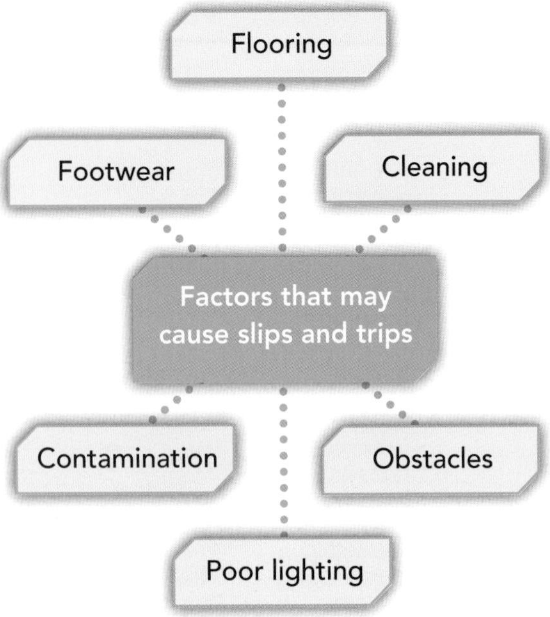

Table 1.5: Key requirements of facilities to avoid slips and trips

Factor	Key requirements
Flooring	• Must be suitable for the type of work activity • Must be cleaned and dried correctly to ensure it doesn't become slippery • Must be fitted correctly • Changes of level should be avoided • Must be maintained in good order
Footwear	• Slip-resistant shoes if required • Footwear policy in the workplace
Cleaning	• Use signs to indicate wet floors • Use barriers to prevent public access while cleaning • Staff should be well trained in use of cleaning chemicals • Equipment should be well maintained
Contamination	• Eliminate the source of the contamination if possible • Clean the contamination • Control the contamination if it cannot be stopped
Obstacles	• Ensure there is a clear walkway • No trailing wires or trip hazards • Keep workstations tidy
Poor lighting	• Lighting needs to be bright enough that obstacles can be seen • Lighting should not be so bright that it impairs vision

Figure 1.3: Factors that cause slips and trips

3.5 Safe methods of manual handling

Manual handling involves lifting and carrying loads. It is governed by the Manual Handling Operations Regulations 1992. The HSE estimates that 38% of all workplace injuries reported to it are caused by poor manual handling and that 1.1 million people in the UK suffer from work-related musculoskeletal disorders. The Manual Handling Operations Regulations lay out a clear process for dealing with the risks:

1. Avoid hazardous manual handling so far as is reasonably practical.

2. Assess any hazardous manual handling that cannot be avoided.

3. Reduce the risk of injury as far as reasonably practical.

Assessment of load

Before you attempt to lift a load, you should assess it to check that you are capable of lifting it. Ask yourself the following:

- How heavy is the load?
- How far do I need to carry it?
- Is it an awkward shape?

When lifting a box (see Figure 1.4) you should take the following into account:

- correct positioning of head, feet and back
- correct positioning of load
- smooth movements
- avoidance of twisting.

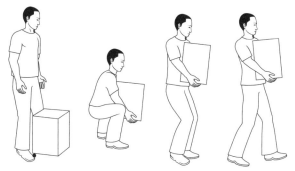

Figure 1.4: Correct positioning when lifting a box

The HSE has produced a document to help you assess the risk associated with lifting/carrying operations. For more information, see www.pearsonhotlinks.co.uk

3.6 Safety signs

Safety signs are used as a warning to employees and members of the public that a hazard may be present. Table 1.6 below outlines the different categories of sign that you might come across in a workplace.

Table 1.6: Safety signs

Colour	Red	Amber	Blue	Green	Red	Various
Meaning	Prohibition; an instruction not to do something	Warning; take precautions, be aware	Mandatory; take a specific action	Safe condition; emergency escape, first aid, exits	Fire fighting; identification and location of fire fighting equipment	Hazchem; information on hazardous chemicals
Example						

3.7 Appropriate reporting procedures for accidents and injuries

RIDDOR is the Reporting of Injuries, Diseases and Dangerous Occurrences Regulation (1995). It places a legal duty on employers, employees and individuals who control premises to report work-related deaths, injuries, accidents and diseases to the HSE.

Reportable and non–reportable injuries under RIDDOR

The HSE provides a clear list of the types of injury and illness that are reportable under RIDDOR. Table 1.7 below shows some of the key reportable issues.

Did you know?

You can find a full and comprehensive list of reportable issues under RIDDOR. Go to www.pearsonhotlinks.co.uk

Table 1.7: Key reportable issues

Injuries	Diseases	Dangerous occurrences
• Fractures • Amputations • Dislocation of the shoulder, hip, knee or spine • Loss of sight • Eye injuries • Unconsciousness caused by asphyxia or exposure to harmful substances or biological agents • Acute illness arising from absorption of any substance by inhalation, ingestion or through the skin • Acute illness requiring medical treatment from exposure to a biological agent or its toxins or infected material	• Poisonings • Skin diseases • Lung diseases • Infections • Occupational cancer • Musculoskeletal disorders • Decompression illness • Hand–arm vibration syndrome	• Failure of load-bearing equipment • Explosion or fire causing suspension of normal work for over 24 hours • Equipment coming into contact with overhead power lines • Malfunction of breathing apparatus • Failure of diving equipment • Collapse or partial collapse of a scaffold • A dangerous substance being conveyed by road being involved in a fire or released

What to record in an accident book

Under health and safety legislation you must keep a record of any RIDDOR occurrence. This is usually done in the form of an accident book, which complies with the Data Protection Act. Accident books generally contain the information required by the HSE about the occurrence and should be completed by the employer or other responsible person. It asks for:

- name, job title and contact details of the person completing the report
- details of the organisation
- details about the incident
- details about the injured person
- details about the injury
- the type of incident
- the number of occurrences
- description of the occurrence
- signatures.

4. Know how to apply the principles of fire safety

Fires in the workplace can cause large-scale financial loss for businesses as well as injury and/or death for their employees and the public. Understanding the principles of fire safety will enable you to keep the public and yourself safe, and potentially reduce the losses faced by your employer.

4.1 Three components of fire

The Fire Triangle

Fire is a chemical reaction between three things:

- **Oxygen** – needed in order for the fire to burn
- **Fuel** – any kind of combustible material such as paper, wood or fabric
- **Heat** – responsible for the initial ignition of the fire and enables the fire to spread.

All of these three things need to be in place for a fire to occur – this is why it is often referred to as the 'fire triangle'. If you remove any one of

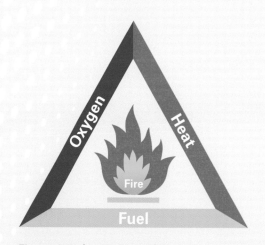

Figure 1.5: the Fire Triangle

the components the fire cannot start. If it has already started and one of the elements is removed the fire will die. For example, when you spray certain types of fire with water, this removes the heat, so that the fire cannot spread.

4.2 Preventing fires

Preventing a fire is far better than dealing with the aftermath of one. Effective fire prevention will save both lives and money. There are some key things that you can do as a member of security personnel to prevent workplace fires.

1. Ensure that sources of fuel and ignition, such as wastepaper bins and lit cigarettes, are controlled. If the workplace has stacks of papers or wood lying around, these are a clear hazard and should be removed or controlled.

2. Many workplaces that use security personnel have valuable resources stored on the premises. Some of these resources, such as wood, paper, textiles or chemicals, can be highly flammable and should be stored safely to prevent fire.

3. Most workplaces will have a large amount of electrical equipment on site. This can range from simple office equipment such as PCs, printers and photocopiers to more complex technical equipment in manufactories. All electrical equipment has the potential to start an electrical fire and should be regularly inspected for safety.

4. One of the common causes of fire in the workplace is the overloading of electrical points. Ensure that you don't have multiple electrical appliances plugged into one socket.

Did you know?

Workplaces should have portable appliance testing (PAT) as part of their health and safety policy to ensure electrical equipment is safe.

4.3 Fire classification

Fires have been classified into different groups depending on the type of fuel they use to burn. Table 1.8 below shows a summary of the classifications.

Table 1.8: Fire classification

Classification	Explanation
Class A	Fires involving freely burning materials such as wood, paper and textiles
Class B	Fires involving flammable liquids such as petrol and diesel
Class C	Fires involving flammable gases such as butane and propane
Class D	Fires involving flammable metals such as sodium or lithium
Class F	Fires involving cooking oils and fat

4.4 Fire extinguishers and fire fighting equipment

Each different classification of fire needs a specific type of fire extinguisher to put it out. It is essential that the right type of extinguisher is used as the wrong extinguisher could actually make the fire worse. The types of extinguisher are:

- water
- foam
- powder
- carbon dioxide (CO_2)
- wet chemical.

The extinguishers have a standard appearance.

Table 1.9 below shows which fire extinguishers should be used for different types of fire.

Table 1.9: Which fire extinguishers to use on different types of fire

Classification	Water	Foam	CO_2	Powder	Wet chemical
Class A	✓	✓		✓	
Class B		✓	✓	✓	
Class C				✓	
Class D				Special powder only	
Class F					✓

Fire blankets

Fire blankets are safety devices designed to extinguish small fires by depriving them of oxygen. They are made from a sheet of fire resistant material, which is placed over the fire to smother it. They have been traditionally used in the home in the case of chip pan fires, but can also be used to wrap around individuals whose clothing has caught fire or put over a person's head if they are escaping a burning building.

Types of sprinkler system

Sprinklers are a system for extinguishing Class A fires in the workplace. They consist of a network of overhead water pipes connected to nozzles that activate when the temperature rises. The water reduces the temperature and smoke, giving occupants of the building more time to evacuate. This can also reduce or extinguish the fire.

Did you know?

There is a mnemonic that can help you remember how to use a fire extinguisher properly. It is **PASS**:
- **P**ull the pin out
- **A**im the nozzle at the base of the fire
- **S**queeze the handle to create the spray
- **S**weep the extinguisher back and forth as you spray the base of the fire.

The two common types of sprinkler system are:

Wet riser – a constantly pressurised water pipe, supplied by a storage tank and pump. All the pipes are constantly filled with water that does not release until a specific temperature range is reached.

Dry riser – a system with pipes full of air initially. The increase in temperature triggers the sprinkler valves to open but they must vent the air inside the pipes before the water can enter. This slight delay means they are often less effective than wet risers during the initial stages of a fire. However they have the advantage of being suitable for unheated parts of a building where wet riser systems might freeze.

4.5 Appropriate responses when discovering a fire

FIRE is a useful mnemonic to remind you what to do if you find a fire:

- **F**ind the fire.

- **I**nform the emergency services about the fire immediately so they can respond appropriately. Quick reporting on your part can save lives.

- **R**estrict the fire from spreading if you can by restricting the fuel and the direction the fire can take. Close doors and windows but do not lock them.

- **E**vacuate the building or **E**xtinguish the fire. If the fire is large and spreading, ensure you and your colleagues get out quickly and safely. If the fire is small enough to be tackled and extinguished, select the right type of extinguisher and, remembering the PASS mnemonic, put the fire out.

4.6 Importance of understanding fire evacuation procedures

It is vitally important that you understand fire evacuation procedures for any premises you are assigned to or are responsible for. There are three key reasons why it is so important:

- To save time in an emergency – If you know the procedures well you can quickly evacuate the workers and the public from a building. This will ultimately save lives and allow the emergency services to deal with the cause of the emergency rather than endangering themselves by rescuing trapped individuals.

- To keep yourself and others safe – Knowing the procedures will enable you to keep yourself and the public safe. Many premises where security personnel operate can be difficult to navigate. Imagine the chaos if a large-scale fire broke out in a large shopping

If the fire is small enough to tackle, select the right type of extinguisher.

mall such as Meadowhall in Sheffield or the Metro Centre in Newcastle. If you know the quickest route out of any given location, you will save lives.

- To assist emergency services – If you deal effectively with an evacuation situation in the minutes before the emergency services arrive, you will be allowing them to focus on the cause of the emergency rather than the evacuation. This can save businesses thousands of pounds, save lives and save the time and resources of the emergency services.

5. Know how to deal with non-fire-related workplace emergencies

5.1 Definition of 'emergency' when used in the workplace

In the workplace it can be very easy to use the word emergency incorrectly. It is a term sometimes used to mean that a task is urgent rather than life threatening. However a real emergency is a situation that is unexpected, threatens safety or causes serious disruption and requires your immediate response.

5.2 Types of workplace emergencies

There are lots of different kinds of emergency that you might encounter while working in the private security industry. Table 1.10 below outlines some of the main ones.

Table 1.10: Descriptions of the kinds of emergency you might encounter while on duty.

Emergency	Description
Power, system or equipment failure	There will be occasions when emergencies are caused by the failure of power or the failure of equipment. For example, in a hospital a power failure could be life threatening, or a failure of equipment, particularly safety equipment, could be extremely hazardous.
Flood	Flooding can be very dangerous and may cost lives and millions of pounds to businesses. Periods of heavy rain can cause high threat levels. It is essential that you are aware of possible flooding risks in your work premises or on your patrol routes.

Activity: Emergencies

Kalum is a security officer working at a large steel factory. During the course of his day he is radioed about the following incidents, all described by his manager as emergencies:

- A reporter has been trying to get access to the plant without authorisation
- A car has broken down and is blocking the main access gate
- A fire has been detected in a rubbish skip
- £20 has gone missing from a worker's wallet
- An odd smell has been detected in a chemical storage room and several staff working in there have complained of vomiting and headaches and one has collapsed.

Considering the definition of an emergency above, which incidents should Kalum treat as real emergencies and respond to immediately?

Table 1.10 (cont.)

Emergency	Description
Serious injury	Many workplaces have a risk of serious injuries due to the nature of the business they do. Door supervisors, vehicle immobilisers and security personnel often work in environments where there is a high risk of interpersonal violence or where heavy machinery is used.
Serious illness	There is always the potential to encounter serious illness in the workplace. Heart attacks are common and you may be the first responder at the scene until the emergency services arrive. Equally, alcohol- and drug-related incidents are not uncommon and can leave individuals with serious illnesses.
Bomb threat	Bomb threats are rare and you may not encounter one in your entire career, but when they do occur they should always be taken seriously as the potential for loss of life and property is high. See page 27 for information on dealing with bomb threats.

5.3 Appropriate responses to workplace emergencies

The action you decide to take when an emergency arises can mean the difference between life and death for you, your colleagues and the public and it can also save your employer's business. There are some key things you can do in any emergency situation to ensure you do your job to the best of your ability:

1. Ensure you follow the correct emergency procedures set down in your health and safety policies or that you have been taught in your training. These procedures will be different depending on the emergency so you must make sure you know them all and can implement them even under pressure.

2. When an emergency happens the very first thing you must do is ensure your own safety. Only when you have established your own safety should you ensure the safety of others. This may sound like an odd thing to do, but if you look at Case study: Jed, Door supervisor on page 27 you will see why this is so important.

3. You must report the incident to the appropriate authorities, including the emergency services, so you can make sure they respond quickly. Any delay could mean lives are lost and premises damaged.

4. You must demonstrate appropriate behaviour at all times. This means remaining calm and in control, encouraging others to remain calm and demonstrating authority if required. There are emergencies where you may feel afraid or under pressure but you cannot afford to show these things until your responsibilities to your colleagues and the public have been fulfilled and everyone is safe.

5. You should know how to make emergency calls. This means being able to quickly contact the people who need to know about an emergency, such as your supervisors and the emergency services, and knowing what information you will need to give over the phone.

Case study: Jed, Door supervisor

Jed is a senior door supervisor with 10 years' experience working in South Yorkshire Clubs. He coordinates a team of 15 door supervisors who operate security for a large Sheffield entertainment venue. A key part of his role is ensuring that all his staff understand safety procedures to ensure both they and the public are kept safe.

"We were having a really busy Friday night in the club, there were around 3000 people in the venue and it had been relatively trouble free. As it came up to closing time, we had a radio call from a bar supervisor to inform us that there was a dispute developing between a drunken customer and the bar staff on an upper floor mezzanine.

Our policy is never to attend a dispute alone, so we always have support if we need it, but on this occasion one of my staff responded to the incident without a colleague. The customer causing the problem was very drunk and aggressive and was refusing to leave. He became violent when my staff member challenged him. By the time we arrived 30 seconds later to assist, there had been a scuffle and my staff member was injured.

We restrained the customer and called 999. The police were very quick to respond as they usually have a strong presence in town on Friday night. My staff member needed four stitches for a head wound, but if he'd followed policy and waited for a colleague he could have avoided it. In my opinion he was lucky to get away with four stitches because it could have been much worse."

Over to you

1. What should the door supervisor have done in these circumstances?

2. Were the door supervisor's actions appropriate? Explain your answer.

3. Can you think of any other situations where you might wait for a colleague before acting?

4. Why is it important to follow set safety policies?

5.4 Procedure for dealing with bomb threat warning calls

In the event that you receive a telephone bomb threat there are several things you can do to assist the police in tracking down the bomb and catching the person responsible. You should ask the following questions and write down the answers. Do not interrupt the caller or you may miss vital details.

- Where is the bomb?
- What time will it go off?
- What does it look like?
- What type of bomb is it?
- Why did you place the bomb?
- What is your name and address?

You should try and note anything you can about the call, such as:

- Is the voice male or female?
- What kind of background noise is there?
- Does the person have an accent?
- Is there anything distinctive about the speech of the caller?
- Is the call from a public telephone?
- What time was the call received?

Once you have received the call you must decide on the action to take:

- Dial 1471 to see if you can trace the caller's number.
- Alert your supervisor and follow instructions.
- Call the police.
- Conduct a search for any unidentified object that should not be there, cannot be explained, or is out of place.
- If you find anything that looks suspicious, do not disturb it.
- Evacuate the premises.

Activity: Dealing with a bomb threat

Mohammed is head of security at a large inner city nightclub. On a busy Saturday night he receives a bomb threat. There are over 3000 people in the club, many of them are under the influence of alcohol and might be difficult to evacuate. Mohammed suspects the call is from a member of staff he sacked earlier in the week as he thinks he recognised the voice of the caller. What actions should Mohammed take?

5.5 Appropriate responses to first aid situations

It is likely that, when working in the private security industry, you will come across first aid situations regularly. It will be a professional advantage if you or your employer pays for a full HSE-approved First Aid at Work qualification. The guidance described below is not a substitute for being properly trained. There are three main aims of first aid:

1. Preserve life
2. Prevent the situation from worsening
3. Promote recovery

Your quick and correct response to a medical incident could save lives. Some of the key issues to remember are covered below.

Did you know?

First aid isn't an exact science; there are occasions where even the most skilled first aider will not be able to save a casualty. All you can do is your best.

First aid priorities

1. Assess the situation – What is happening? Is there an immediate cause? Will you require additional help? Remain calm. Look for clues that might help establish what has happened. Ask witnesses.

2. Protect yourself and the casualty from any further danger – Could the incident happen to other people? Can you remove the hazard safely? Is the casualty in further danger?

3. Comfort and reassure the casualty – What is their name? Be calm and confident.

4. Provide treatment – Treat the cause of the injury or, if the injury is severe, try and prevent worsening.

5. Call for medical help if required – Call 999 and provide sufficient details to help the paramedic crew.

If you come across a casualty who is unresponsive, you should seek additional assistance immediately, by shouting or radioing for a colleague or member of the public to call 999. If you come across a casualty when you are alone and without assistance, you should call 999 before you deal with the incident so the emergency services can be on their way as fast as possible. You should then ensure the casualty has an open airway by using a 'head tilt' or 'chin lift'. This is where you place your hand on the casualty's forehead and gently tilt the head back or, with your fingers under the point of the casualty's chin, you gently lift to open the airway.

The next step is to check if the unresponsive casualty is breathing. To do this you should look at the chest and abdomen to see if you can observe breathing movements, listen for sounds of breathing or feel for the movement of air on your cheek, or feel for breathing motions in the chest. If the casualty is breathing you would normally carry out a secondary survey and place them in the recovery position.

In order to conduct a secondary survey you would normally check the following:

- Do a quick head-to-toe check for bleeding, especially in hidden areas such as the bottom of the back and neck where blood can pool, and control any bleeding you find.

- Look for any clues to injury such as bruising, swelling or deformity, particularly in the head and neck area.

- Check the collarbones and ribs and check shoulders appear level.

- Check the abdomen is not distended or swollen or misshapen as a result of damage to the pelvis.

- Check the limbs for bleeding and fractures. Pay particular attention to looking for medical bracelets or needle marks on the casualty.

- Check for anything in the pockets that might injure the casualty when you move them into the recovery position. Be careful as there may be sharp objects in the pockets and ensure you have a witness if you remove anything from the pockets.

- Loosen tight clothing.

- Place the casualty in the recovery position (see Figure 1.6), if this is appropriate. Remember that if the casualty has a head or spinal injury you should not move them.

Figure 1.6: The recovery position.

Activity: Secondary survey

Ask a colleague or a family member to pretend to be your casualty and conduct a secondary survey on them.

If the casualty is not breathing you should ensure the paramedics are on their way and commence cardio-pulmonary resuscitation (CPR). CPR consists of chest compressions to force the heart to circulate blood around the body and rescue breaths to oxygenate the blood; the ratio is 30 compressions to 2 rescue breaths.

Bleeding

If you come across a casualty who is bleeding from a wound or injury your priority is to stop the bleeding and prevent the casualty going into shock. The mnemonic to help you remember how to treat bleeding is SEEP:

- **S**it or lie the casualty down in a position that is appropriate for the location and treatment of the injury. Blood loss can cause unconsciousness so it is better to have the casualty in a safe position where they cannot fall far and hurt themselves further.

- **E**xamine the wound; look for foreign objects such as shards of glass or metal.

- **E**levate the injured area above the heart so you can use gravity to slow the bleeding.

- **P**ressure can be used either directly or indirectly to stem the bleeding.

6. Understand the principles of effective communication and customer care in the private security industry

Effective communication and customer service are at the heart of an effective private security industry. This part of the course discusses the main forms of communication and the problems that can arise and looks at different types of customer and how they can be served.

6.1 Elements of the communication process

Communication is about conveying your messages to other people clearly and effectively and receiving information that others are sending you. This is called the sender–receiver model of communication. Not all messages are verbal or easily understood so it is important to have a firm understanding of this area before you being working in the security sector.

6.2 Methods of verbal and non-verbal communication

Non-verbal communication is the process of sending wordless messages to others. You might think that would be very difficult but in actual fact humans communicate non-verbally most of the time. One study indicated that up to 93% of the communication we receive is non-verbal. Table 1.11 describes the ways we give this information.

Table 1.11: Types of non-verbal communication

Non-verbal communication	Description
Gestures	Gestures, such as pointing or nodding, can convey a range of messages accurately without the need for words. If you asked the way to the nearest phone and the receiver of the question pointed, it would be clear to you where the phone was.
Eye contact	Eye contact is essential in building and maintaining trust in communication. It can also indicate that you are the focus of someone's attention which can either be a benefit or a threat.
Facial expression	Human faces are very mobile and we use a variety of expressions to indicate our message such as frowns, smiles, raised eyebrows, wide eyes, open mouth, pursed lips and so on.
Stance	Your stance can indicate confidence or fear or aggression just by a subtle repositioning of your weight and body.
Paralanguage	This is the pitch, tone and intonation of speech. It can indicate sarcasm, irony or humour. It also includes non-speech verbal sounds such as grunts, shushes, sobs and whispers.

Understanding non-verbal communication can help you identify possible sources of threat to yourself and the public, identify suspicious behaviour and spot signs of distress in others. Reading and writing are also forms of non-verbal communication although they still use language to convey their message.

Verbal communication

The other 7% of communication is verbal and this primarily consists of speaking and listening skills. It can be surprisingly difficult to create a clear line of communication using speaking and listening as there can be many barriers to the message.

Activity: Non-verbal communication

Genna is a security officer in a large shopping centre. During the course of her shift she sees the following types of behaviour:
- A child alone and crying
- A middle-aged man making direct eye contact with a woman and standing very close to her in an aggressive manner
- An elderly lady looking confused
- A group of young people nudging each other and giggling outside the entrance to a jewellery shop.

Using just the non-verbal cues you have been given what could be going on in each of the scenarios that Genna sees? What actions should she take in each case?

6.3 Barriers to communication

It can be very difficult to create clear communication as there are many things that can distort the message. Table 1.12 below outlines some of the most common barriers.

Table 1.12: Barriers to communication

Barrier	Description
Physical	There can be physical barriers to communication such as equipment failure, e.g. radios, telephones. There can be a physical separation between sender and receiver in terms of distance, making communication difficult. Background noise can distort the message and lighting can make it very difficult to interpret body language or facial expression.
Attitude	Your attitude directly influences how you send and receive messages. If you don't like the sender or receiver you are likely to make incorrect assumptions about the message or become complacent that you already know what the message is going to be. This can have serious consequences.
Emotion	Emotion can make communication very difficult. It is difficult to get a clear message through to a receiver if there is anger, stress, fear or nervousness present. In the security sector there will be occasions where you will have to deal with high levels of emotion and still get your message across or understand the message given to you.
Linguistic	There can be significant linguistic barriers to communication such as the use of slang or jargon or if the sender or receiver has a very strong accent or there is a language barrier. This can lead to a very unclear message which cannot be interpreted correctly, leading to potential confusion.
Organisational	The organisation can also be a direct barrier to communication if it doesn't have clear lines of report and communication or if it doesn't make clear job roles and responsibilities.

Activity: Communication

You are working as security for a large international sporting event in the UK. Each nation has brought with it a small security contingent and it is your role to ensure that all of these small foreign security teams can integrate and communicate with the larger UK team. What barriers to communication might you face and what steps could you take to overcome them?

6.4 Importance of effective communication in the workplace

Effective communication starts with choosing the right language and communication method for the message. Delivering a message in French or in semaphore may not be an effective communication method if your recipient doesn't know that form of communication. You need to ensure your message is clear and then check the recipient has understood what you intended them to understand.

Effective communication is essential in most service sectors as you deal directly with the public and clients during the majority of your working day; the security sector is no different. It is therefore essential that you master the basics of essential communication in order for you to do your job well. It will ensure your organisation is operationally effective and you work well with your team. It also ensures your customers get the service they are paying for.

6.5 Types of customers and their needs

In the security industry it is important to know your customers and provide them with the service they need. Generally you will find you encounter the following types of customer:

- **Internal** – Some security staff do not work for a security company; they work directly for the agency that employs them. Therefore, their main focus will be on the customers internal to the organisation. For example, if you were employed as security by a college, your customers would be the staff and students who use the college on a daily basis.

- **External** – For security staff employed by a security company which then services other businesses and industries, the focus will be on external customers.

- **Direct** – Direct customers are the ones who are directly purchasing or paying for your services.

- **Indirect** – Indirect customers operate through a third party or intermediary and do not deal with security companies or personnel directly.

Customers have a variety of individual needs that you have to consider when carrying out your duties. If you are working in a large company, organisation or venue it is likely you will encounter speakers of other languages, and individuals with visual or auditory impairment, physical difficulties such as mobility problems or learning difficulties.

Case study: Sam, Security officer at a college

"We have a team of about 30 officers to watch over three different campuses, 1000 staff and nearly 10,000 students. It's a tall order, but it's even more of a challenge when you consider all the students are very different. For example, we have a lot of students who don't have English as their first language, students with learning difficulties and students with disabilities. We give all our staff very clear training about what is expected of them in terms of dealing with the students and we have put a couple of the staff through some basic language courses at the college so we can communicate better. We also arranged for one of the academic staff to give us a seminar on dealing with individuals with learning disabilities. It's quite a challenge, but I enjoy the work as it is varied and I come into contact with different people every day."

Over to you

1. What challenges does working in a large and diverse organisation bring?

2. Why is it important to have training on dealing with different customers?

3. What are the possible consequences of being poorly trained?

6.6 Principles of customer care

There are some basic principles which everyone who is dealing with customers regularly should be aware of. It is really important to build a strong and positive rapport with customers. This can be done in some very simple ways such as making sure you acknowledge them rather than ignore them and communicating information to them pleasantly and with a smile if appropriate. Consider how you like to be treated when you are a customer and make that your standard of behaviour. There are six golden rules to follow:

1. **Acknowledge the customer** – smile at them, say hello and make sure they know they have your attention.

2. **Establish the customer's needs** – find out what they need and ensure you have understood their requests properly.

3. **Put yourself in the customer's position** – how does the customer feel and how would you feel in that situation?

4. **Accept responsibility** – the customer has come to you, do not pass them off elsewhere because you have other things to do. Take responsibility for getting them what they need or advise them how to get assistance if you don't have the skills or knowledge to deal with that at the time.

5. **Involve the customer in the solution** – how would the customer like to see the problem resolved?

6. **See it through** – ensure you do what you said you were going to do.

Just checking

1. What are the main purposes of the security industry?

2. What are the main functions of the SIA?

3. What are the key differences between civil and criminal law?

4. List the eight principles of the Data Protection Act.

5. What is the name of the key piece of legislation governing health and safety in the workplace?

6. List the typical hazards that can cause trips, slips and falls.

7. What injuries are and are not reportable under RIDDOR?

8. What are the three components of a fire?

9. Describe the five common fire classifications.

10. How would you define an emergency?

11. In the case of a bomb threat, what questions would you ask the caller?

12. What are common barriers to communication?

13. Why is effective communication important?

14. What types of customer are you likely to come into contact with?

15. What are the six golden rules when dealing with customer issues?

Cortez Marshall

Senior security officer in a local government office

The city centre offices I work in deal with all kinds of council issues, from social housing repairs to benefits claims. It can be a very busy and noisy environment and we were finding we were having lots of security incidents at busy times such as Saturday morning. We reviewed the way the space was set up and spoke with customers who were having difficulties and it became clear that the security we had set up to protect staff was actually having a detrimental impact. The safety glass in front of the council workers was impairing how well they could hear the members of the public and was leading to misunderstandings and frustrations. We had created a single waiting area for everyone for ease of surveillance, but the noise level made effective communication impossible. We decided to redesign the space to make communication easier and faster by removing the security glass, structuring different waiting areas for different issues and ensuring security staff were seen as a source of support to the public not as a threat. We have recorded 76% less security incidents per month as a result of the changes.

Over to you

1. What were the key issues with effective communication in this situation?

2. Why would not being able to communicate effectively cause difficulties for the security team?

3. Can you think of any premises you know where the design could be a problem for security?

4. If you were Cortez what would you have done about the situation?

2DS Working as a door supervisor

Working in the private security industry as a licensed door supervisor is a fascinating, challenging and highly rewarding career. The role of the door supervisor is to provide an effective presence at a venue, to assist customers and members of the public, deter crime and resolve conflict – though, thankfully, not always at the same time.

The aim of this unit is to explore what you will need to know about the objectives, roles and responsibilities of a door supervisor and to understand how vital it is to operate within the law. You will also cover all the relevant issues concerning current standards and legislation and the organisations responsible for them. This unit also covers arrest procedures, searching venues and individuals, drug awareness, licensing laws and equal opportunities.

Learning outcomes

After completing this unit you should:

1. understand the behaviour appropriate for individual door supervisors
2. understand elements of civil and criminal law relevant to door supervisors
3. understand admission policies and search procedures
4. understand the powers of citizen's arrest and related procedures
5. understand relevant drug legislation and its relevance to the role of the door supervisor
6. understand incident recording and crime scene preservation
7. understand licensing law and social responsibility relating to licensed premises
8. understand safety and security issues relevant to door supervisors.

Security alert!

Secure your future

Think about the personal attributes that will help you to do your job as a door supervisor. Make a list of five attributes that you think are positive and three that you think would be negative. Think about things such as how you dress, how you greet customers, what kind of language you use on the job and how fit and alert you are.

1. Understand the behaviour appropriate for individual door supervisors

1.1 SIA's standards of behaviour for door supervisors

Behavioural standards are a combination of personality traits, skills, knowledge, training and formal legislation which work in unison to ensure that organisations and individuals conduct themselves in a manner which produces the highest level of service.

As an individual your personal effectiveness and the manner in which you communicate are important contributing factors. Also of importance is your ability to work within a team and how you present yourself.

Having the necessary skills, qualifications and a valid SIA licence are mandatory requirements for a door supervisor. However, there is also a wide range of personality attributes that can be combined to enable you to stand out as a true professional in the industry.

Being understanding, patient and tolerant in stressful situations is enormously beneficial to all concerned, especially if you are dealing with a large group where several people are expressing themselves at the same time or may be under the influence of drugs and alcohol.

Listening carefully without displaying **discrimination**, bias or favouritism will allow you to rapidly establish the cause of the problem, which can then be dealt with accordingly.

Behavioural standards are an important part of everyday society. Our own personal behavioural standards determine how we interact with others and can affect our methods of communication, how we assist others, how we conduct ourselves and how we deal with and resolve conflict. Behavioural standards can vary from person to person and can be affected by upbringing, social status and personal disposition – people can be upbeat, laid back or moody on different days. Likewise, the behavioural standards of companies and organisations can often be determined by their customer service policies, staff training and

Key term

Discrimination – treating an individual less favourably than another individual based on his or her age, accent, social status, religion, sex, sexual orientation, race, country of origin, colour, ethnicity or disability

development as well as things like annual profits, market competition and the economy.

Due to these variations in personal, social and economic behavioural standards it is important for organisations to implement a structured and well-organised Charter of Behavioural Standards, and the SIA (Security Industry Authority) is responsible for this in the security industry.

1.2 Why are standards of behaviour required?

Prior to the existence of the SIA, it was possible for anybody to work in the private security industry, which could mean that those in positions of trust and responsibility had criminal records and / or no training to assist them to undertake their duties in a safe, conscientious and professional manner. In some circumstances, this led to abuse of trust and a lack of appropriate care shown to customers and members of the public.

The outcome of the SIA standards of behaviour is a safer environment for the public and for door supervisors to work in, which enhances the reputation of the private security industry and the careers of individuals within the industry. These raised standards of professional conduct have the impact of increasing public confidence in the sector and promoting positive relationships with the public, maintaining good working relationships with the police service and improving the reputation of individual venues and the sector as a whole. All of these key issues help to strengthen the professional image of the industry and generate additional revenue on the door.

1.3 Requirements relating to SIA licensing

It is a criminal offence to undertake the licensable activities of a door supervisor without an SIA licence. A licence is required for anyone who undertakes manned guarding activities in relation to a licensed premises. The SIA states that a door supervisor licence is required if you are performing this guarding activity on behalf of yourself or your employer or if your services are supplied for the purposes of or in connection with any contract to a consumer.

The following standards are set out for the SIA in their Door Supervisor specifications. A door supervisor should at all times:

- wear clothing which is smart, presentable, easily identifies the individual as a door supervisor, and is in accordance with the employer's guidelines

- wear his/her SIA licence on the outside of their clothing while on duty, displaying the photograph side. The licence must not be altered.

You should wear clothing which is smart, presentable and easily identifies you as a door supervisor.

Did you know?

The SIA's main responsibilities include:
- The mandatory licensing of individuals wishing to work in the Private Security Industry
- To continually review, assess and regulate the Private Security Industry in order to reduce criminality, raise standards and actively encourage and promote the highest level of service
- To monitor the activities and overall effectiveness of individuals and organisations within the industry through inspections and continually updating and improving current legislation
- To set standards of conduct and training at the highest levels so as to ensure the safety and well-being of the Industry's employers, employees, customers and clients.

It is your role to ensure that the people entering the premises are legitimate customers and the venue does not breach its overall capacity.

Activity: Why have standards?

Choose four roles from the table and discuss why you think these standards are important to have. What could happen if you were not there to carry out these duties.

You must notify the SIA if:

- you lose your licence
- you are convicted of a criminal offence, cautioned or warned for a relevant offence
- there is any change to your address or your legal right to work in the UK.

The SIA operates a system of approved contractors. This is where the SIA inspects providers of security services and organisations that meet agreed standards are approved to operate as contractors of security services. The scheme is designed to raise standards and to help the private security industry to develop new business opportunities. The SIA can inspect organisations that have staff carrying out licensable activities on a random basis to ensure staff are appropriately registered and displaying their SIA licence. SIA spot checks can occur at any time so it is good practice to ensure you have it displayed where it can be seen (unless you are engaging in security activities which require anonymity, such as close protection). Licenses are routinely returned to the SIA for updating or renewal if they become damaged or defaced. You will also be required to return your licence to the SIA if it becomes clear that you obtained the licence fraudulently or you are not permitted to work in the UK.

1.4 The role and objectives of the door supervisor

A door supervisor needs to be flexible and adaptable and be able to deal with any situation they come across in the course of their day-to-day working life. However, there are common roles and key tasks that you will be expected to deal with on a more frequent basis.

Table 2DS.1: Roles of a door supervisor.

Role	Description
Control of access	It is your role to ensure that the people entering the premises you are responsible for are legitimate customers and the venue does not breach its overall capacity. This role also includes ensuring customers are not carrying prohibited items such as weapons or drugs when they enter the premises.
Enforcement	You will be required to enforce the law, your company's policies and the venue's entry conditions as a key part of your role. This may include preventing prohibited items coming into the premises as mentioned above, ensuring a dress code is applied and removing people who have broken the law or the rules of the venue.

Table 2DS.1 (cont.)

Role	Description
Ensuring safety and security	A key part of your role as a door supervisor is ensuring the safety and security of the venue and the staff and customers within it. This includes routine safety measures such as weapon and drugs searches, as well as dealing with alcohol-related violence and providing first aid when required. However it also includes response to serious emergency incidents such as bomb threats, terrorist activity and firearms incidents.
Prevention of crime, disorder and unacceptable behaviour	The prevention of crime and disorder is an essential element of the job of a door supervisor. It is likely that you will work as part of a well-trained team along with the police to reduce disorder both inside and outside your venue.

1.5 Key qualities of a door supervisor

In order to be an effective door supervisor you will need a range of key skills and qualities which will enable you to provide the public with the service they expect and help you to maintain the good reputation of your employer.

Oral communication – You need to be able to communicate verbally with your customers. Your job role is all about customer interaction and you are often the public face of your venue. As well as ensuring the premises and public are safe you also play a key marketing role. If your communication is poor, people may choose to avoid your club or pub meaning a loss of revenue for your employer. You will also struggle to resolve conflict if you cannot communicate verbally.

Interpersonal and teamworking skills – Door supervisors rarely work alone: it is likely you will be part of a team of door supervisors. You will also be part of the general staff of the venue including bar staff, kitchen staff, managers and cleaning staff who must all work together to ensure premises are fit for the public. You will rely heavily on your colleagues to alert you to potential conflict and to support you if you are dealing with conflict. Therefore sound teamworking skills and interpersonal behaviour will be critical to your success in the role.

Quick thinking and decisiveness – In a busy entertainment venue, emergency or conflict situations can occur without warning in the space of seconds. You must be flexible and adaptable enough to make decisions quickly and respond to situations on the spot. If you cannot do this, conflict may escalate into outright violence and an emergency could go unchecked leaving people injured – or worse – as a result.

Activity: Your qualities

Consider the following qualities:
- Interpersonal skills
- Oral communication
- Teamworking
- Quick thinking
- Decisiveness
- Politeness
- Courtesy
- Assertiveness
- Calmness under pressure
- Honesty
- Fairness
- Observation skills

Rate yourself on each of these skills with 1 being very poor and 5 being excellent. Which of these qualities are your main strengths? Which of these qualities will you need to develop before you can become a successful door supervisor?

Do you have all the qualities that make a good door supervisor?

Politeness and courtesy – Remember that you are the public face of your venue. You are the one the customer may see before anyone else. If you are rude or aggressive the customers will go elsewhere with a consequent loss of revenue to your employer. Treat people coming to your venue as you would wish to be treated if you were on a night out and always treat your customers with courtesy and politeness even in the most difficult of circumstances.

Assertiveness and calmness under pressure – As a door supervisor you will need to be assertive about what standards of behaviour and conduct you expect from your customers and have the ability to remain calm even when aggressively challenged. Aggression and tension shown by you can escalate a conflict situation whereas calmness can often defuse it.

Honesty and fairness – These are skills required in all jobs where you are dealing with the public, including the work of a door supervisor. You will be dealing with legal matters and the police on a regular basis and it is important that you report the facts in a fair and honest way if you are to help uphold the law. You will also be dealing with conflict and being fair to all concerned is a good tool to use in conflict resolution.

Observation skills – The ability to observe a crowded environment and notice anything which looks out of place, or identify a trouble spot before it happens, is a key quality required of a door supervisor. By observing carefully you can prevent issues before they arise and save yourself time and your employer money in the process.

2. Understand elements of civil and criminal law relevant to door supervisors

In order to do your job effectively you will need to know how civil and criminal law relate to you in the execution of your duties. If you are unaware of the law you may find yourself in court defending your own actions and possibly face punishment because of your lack of knowledge. This is particularly important when examining the use of force. The information in this chapter is based on the laws of England and Wales.

2.1 The law and how it relates to use of force

Criminal Law Act 1967

There was a time when door supervisors, or 'bouncers' as they were then called, had a very bad reputation for excessive use of violence. Thankfully those days are now gone and the industry is highly trained and professionalised, particularly in the use of force. The key piece of legislation which door supervisors should be aware of is the Criminal Law Act 1967. Section three of this act states that:

'Any person may use such force as is reasonable in the circumstances in the prevention of a crime or in effecting or assisting in the lawful arrest of offenders or suspected offenders or of persons unlawfully at large.'

Therefore door supervisors (or indeed any member of the public) may use reasonable force to prevent a crime or lawfully arrest an offender. As a door supervisor you have no more powers to use force than any other member of the public and you should always remember this. If you use excessive force you will be liable to prosecution and very likely lose your job as well as face fines or a possible prison sentence.

Case study: Andrew Lee

In 2009 door supervisor Andrew Lee was charged with causing grievous bodily harm to student John Jones. Mr Jones and his girlfriend had attended a fancy dress night out in the KAOS club in Southampton. Towards the end of the evening the pair began to argue and Andrew Lee stepped in to eject Mr Jones from the club.

A tussle ensued and Mr Jones was placed in a full nelson hold by Mr Lee and was dragged towards the exit. Unfortunately the pair fell and as a result of the hold and the fall Mr Jones suffered a broken neck which left him paralysed and in a wheelchair. Mr Lee was convicted of causing grievous bodily harm to Mr Jones and sentenced to four years' imprisonment. The prosecution commented that Lee's actions in this instance were 'unnecessary' and 'unreasonable' and directly led to the terrible injuries suffered by Mr Jones.

Over to you

1. Why is an understanding of the law on the use of force needed by door supervisors?

2. What could have been done differently in this situation by the door supervisor?

3. What are the consequences of being unaware of the law or choosing to ignore it?

How you use force and the consequences of your actions will be critical to your success in your job. There are dedicated firms of solicitors who target potential assault cases by door supervisors so it is essential you know exactly where you stand and never cross the line into unreasonable or unnecessary use of force. It is also important that where you have no choice but to use force you should always be supported by another colleague to ensure you have a witness and to ensure the risk of injury to your customer and to yourself is minimal.

Key terms

Reasonable – Was it reasonable to use force in a given situation? Had every other option been tried and exhausted? Could the situation have been left? Was force ultimately the only available option in the circumstances?

Necessary – Was the action necessary? Could the person have been persuaded to comply by other means? Was force required to prevent a crime or protect others?

Proportional – Was the amount of force used appropriate to the situation or was it excessive?

The difficulty comes in defining what is **reasonable**, **necessary** and **proportional**. Essentially, this is a matter for your judgement at the scene of the incident, but it could ultimately be decided by a court of law. You need to consider issues such as the gender of the person, their size, the nature of the incident, if there is a weapon involved, their age and whether alcohol or drugs are involved. You need to use the absolute minimum of force as a last resort only in order for your actions to be considered reasonable, proportionate and necessary. Unit 4 on physical intervention goes into this in more detail.

2.2 Different types of assault as defined by the law

In criminal and civil law there are different types of assault which you need to be aware of if you may be required to use force as part of your job (see Table 2DS.2 below). This is an important part of your job knowledge as you may be working in an environment where people use alcohol and illegal substances, and this can lead them to make unwise choices in their personal behaviour and conduct, leading to possible instances of violence and assault.

Table 2DS.2: Types of assault

Type of assault	Description
Common assault	Common assault is covered under section 39 of the Criminal Justice Act 1988. It is the least serious form of assault and normally leaves no visible injury. It may involve action such as pushing and shoving, but in law an assault is also when one person makes another fear that violence will be used against them – even if it subsequently isn't. Common assault is a summary offence and carries a possible six month prison sentence and £5000 fine although these maximum sentences are rare.
Actual bodily harm (ABH)	ABH is covered by section 47 of the Offences Against the Person Act. Unlike common assault where there is usually no visible injury, ABH is an assault that leaves visible injuries such as bruising, bite marks or scratches. ABH carries a maximum sentence of five years.
Grievous bodily harm (GBH)	GBH is covered by sections 18 and 20 of the Offences Against the Person Act. In this type of assault there is usually very serious harm done to the victim in the form of broken bones, internal injuries or open wounds such as you might find in a stabbing. The sentence received for GBH is influenced by the intention of the aggressor. If the aggressor breaks a victim's ribs with violence but had not specifically wanted to cause the damage they would be charged under section 20 (Causing GBH) and face a possible 5-year prison term. If the aggressor had deliberately set out to break the person's ribs they would be charged under section 18 (Inflicting GBH) and could in theory face a life jail term, although the maximum sentence is rarely given.
Sexual assault	A sexual assault is defined under section 3 of the Sexual Offences Act 2003 as a person touching anyone else sexually without the person's consent. It carries with it a maximum sentence of 10 years' imprisonment.
Rape	Under the Sexual Offences Act 2003 it is illegal for a male to penetrate the vagina, anus or mouth of another male or female with his penis without consent. The consequences of a rape conviction can be up to life imprisonment.

2.3 Offences against property that a door supervisor may come across

As well as dealing with incidents of violence and assault it is very likely that you will have to deal with other types of offences related to your venue, such as criminal damage and theft.

- **Criminal damage** – the primary law relating to criminal damage is the Criminal Damage Act 1971 and it is defined as occurring when a person, without lawful excuse, destroys or damages any property belonging to another or is reckless as to whether any such property will be destroyed or damaged.

- **Theft** – the taking of another person's property without their consent with the intention to permanently deprive them of it. The laws on theft are generally covered by the Theft Act 1968.

- **Trespass** – most commonly means to interfere with a person's land, for instance, by entering the land without permission. Trespass is not a criminal matter and you cannot be prosecuted for it in a criminal court.

These crimes are not unique to entertainment venues, but the involvement of alcohol can often create an environment where such offences happen more frequently than in other venue types.

2.4 What to do when a law is broken

At some point in the course of your duties you will have to deal with a situation where the law has been broken and you will have to examine the options open to you in terms of how you deal with the situation. The list below looks at your possible options.

- Ask the customer to leave – you could decide the best way forward is to get the customer off your premises, in which case asking them to leave is your first step. The problem with this is that it may simply move the criminal behaviour elsewhere which doesn't serve justice in the long term.

- Forced ejection and right to evict – if the customer is unwilling to leave of their own volition you have the option to force the matter and eject them from the premises. Remember that any use of force must be reasonable, necessary and proportionate and always ensure you have the support of colleagues when taking force-related actions.

- Arrest – you could choose to opt for a citizen's arrest which is explained on page 54.

Criminal damage is when a person who, without lawful excuse, destroys or damages any property belonging to another.

- Confiscating relevant items – if the activity relates to prohibited items such as weapons or illegal substances you could choose to confiscate the items and hand them over to the relevant authorities.

- Notifying the police – with any criminal offence you have the option to call the police and have them deal with the individuals concerned.

3. Understanding admission policies and search procedures

As a door supervisor you will be expected to know the admissions policy of your organisation and apply it to your work, including access to premises and the protocols for searching members of the public.

3.1 The importance of admission policies

All venues that you work in ought to have a clear and unambiguous admissions policy. The policy exists to uphold the standards your venue wants to see in its customers and provides a measure of consistency and fairness for door supervisors. You cannot be accused of unfairness or prejudice if you consistently and accurately follow the policy. These policies therefore protect you as well as your venue. In general they are used for three main reasons:

- **Managing customer expectations** – If the policy is clearly visible and accessible to everyone, people will know what to expect in terms of wait times, search procedures and dress codes. This can help remove the potential for conflict. For example, if someone has waited for an hour to get into your venue only to be told they don't meet the dress requirements it is likely they will be very unhappy. If the policy was clearly accessible and visible when they began queuing they could have made the choice to go elsewhere.

- **Deterring unacceptable behaviour** – A clear policy sets out the standards of acceptable behaviour required from your customers. If they have read and understood what is required of them and they know the consequences of not meeting those standards of behaviour they may be more likely to refrain from unacceptable behaviour.

- **Justifying refusals / ejections** – The policy also provides you with clear justification when you refuse entry to a member of the public or eject someone because their behaviour falls short of the required standards. A clear policy removes the decision from the individual door supervisor and makes the actions seem less personal, which can reduce the incidence of conflict.

A policy provides clear justification when removing someone from the premise if their behaviour falls short of acceptable standards

3.2 Common areas that can be included in an admissions policy

Admissions policies in most entertainment venues have common elements that you will be required to check or enforce (see Table 2DS.3).

Table 2DS.3: The elements of admissions policies that you will need to check or enforce at entertainment venues

Element of admission	Description
Behaviour / physical state	You will be required to check that the people you are allowing into the venue are in a fit state and demonstrating appropriate standards of behaviour. Refusals can be made to people who are already very intoxicated or who are aggressive.
Entrance fee	In order to access many venues there is a cover charge or entrance fee. If a customer refuses to pay they will not be allowed entry.
Search conditions	In order for entry to be granted many venues require the customer to agree to a voluntary search of their person and property. Not agreeing to a search equals no access.
Age and acceptable proofs	Many entertainment venues have age restrictions as they serve alcohol on the premises. Generally in the UK this is 18 years of age. Policies can request that proof of age is shown in order to gain access.

3.3 Reasons for searching premises

The importance of searching both individuals and venues can never be over-emphasised and it will be your responsibility as a door supervisor to conduct thorough searches efficiently, courteously and with total confidence and expertise. Searching premises is carried out for clear organisational purposes such as the safety and security of the public or the premises. Common search purposes are described in Table 2DS.4.

Table 2DS.4: Reasons for carrying out searches.

Search reasons	Description
Ensuring evacuation routes are clear	In the event of an emergency it is extremely important that evacuation routes and exits are kept clear and free of obstructions so that people can be evacuated in safety. In the event of a fire in a busy pub or club, if the evacuation routes aren't clear the consequences could be disastrous.
Checks of safety equipment	It is routine to check premises to ensure safety equipment such as alarms, fire extinguishers, sprinkler systems and CCTV are all working as intended and support the safety of the customers and staff in the venue.
Suspicious objects	Searches of premises might turn up all sorts of unusual or suspicious objects such as discarded drug paraphernalia and hidden weapons. Unearthing and confiscating these objects keeps customers and staff safer.
Ensuring relevant areas are secure	A key role you might undertake is ensuring back access to the club or pub is kept secure. There can often be thousands of pounds in cash and consumables such as food and alcohol kept in store on a busy weekend night and securing the areas where these goods are kept is very important if the venue is to avoid being a victim of theft.

Case study: Routine searches

Jamilla has been a door supervisor at a busy Bristol club for the last eighteen months.

"We always do routine checks and searches at the beginning of a shift, at the end of the night and at certain points in between. You'd be amazed at the kind of things we find. You get the usual stuff like bags of pills stuffed in toilet cisterns and the odd knife hidden under chairs – we do really thorough searches of all our customers on the way in, but the nature of the business is that some things will slip through the net which is why the premises search is so important.

The most unusual things we have found included £10,000 in cash hidden under a small ledge under one of the upper floor bars, a homemade firearm in a toilet and, shockingly, we once found a four month old baby fast asleep in a car seat! The mother had come out with friends after failing to find a babysitter, had a few drinks and gone home without him. We still have no idea how she managed to sneak him in – we called social services and the police in on that one. There is no such thing as routine in this job!"

Over to you

1. Why do you need premises searches if you are also doing person searches at the door?

2. What are the benefits of searching your venue?

3. What are the consequences of not searching a venue regularly?

3.4 How to search people and their property

It is very important that you observe the law and keep to the highest standards when searching individuals and, therefore, it is essential that you know your rights.

Rules governed by law state that:

- a door supervisor, as a member of the public, has no legal power or special authority to search persons or property

- the searching of an individual **can only** be conducted with his or her prior permission

- a door supervisor **must never** subject any individual to a search using force.

Most people will be happy to comply with a search request but, as with all searches, it is necessary to abide by the following criteria:

- **S**eek permission
- **E**mpathise with the person being searched
- **A**ct in a professional manner at all times
- **R**espond in a polite and courteous manner
- **C**ontrol the search
- **H**elp and assist where difficulties are experienced.

Due to the physical nature of a search, certain individuals may feel intimidated, exposed and even threatened. For this reason, as a qualified and professional door supervisor, you will need to use your communication skills to reassure the individual that it is a practical, impersonal and necessary procedure which will ensure the safety and security of themselves and other members of the public as well as you and your colleagues.

Searching individuals can be a very difficult undertaking and can cause distress and embarrassment to those being searched. There are elements of best practice you should consider during all your searching activities.

It is important also to remember that men should only ever be searched by male door supervisors and, likewise, women are to be searched only by female door supervisors. Same-sex searches reduce the risk of inappropriate conduct or spurious allegations against door supervisors and reduce levels of embarrassment.

Female customers are to be searched only by female door supervisors.

Before searching it is worth considering the merits of self-search. Asking someone to empty their pockets or open their handbag is far preferable to you having to do it and you are likely to find people more cooperative in this form of searching. When you do have to search an individual you should ensure that the facilities are suitable and the individual's privacy is protected from other members of the public or other staff. It is also important to ensure that witnesses are present at a search to reduce the likelihood of false allegations of misconduct being made against either party. It is important to maintain an accurate record of any searches so that if any queries or complaints are made there is a full and accurate record available for reference.

3.5 Difference between general, random and specific searches

There are, essentially, three types of individual search:

- General – this is a policy whereby every visitor to a venue is routinely searched prior to entry.

- Random – in this category visitors are searched at random. The primary aim of this type of search is to act as a deterrent.

- Specific – an individual is searched if there is a belief that they are in possession of any unauthorised or illegal item.

3.6 Hazards involved with conducting searches and appropriate precautions

Although the vast majority of searches pass without incident, you will be confronted with a number of hazards in your working life that you need to be able to deal with both effectively and efficiently. These hazards may include a verbal or physical assault prior to, or during the search. Needle stick injuries are another hazard. You may also be subjected to allegations of assault and 'planting'.

Needle stick injuries are easily avoided by wearing appropriate gloves. If you do face allegations of 'planting' you should call for assistance in the first instance so that as much information (witness statements, CCTV footage, etc.) can be collected as quickly as possible. A witness for both sides will help eliminate this risk.

Prior to conducting the search you should ask each individual the following questions:

- Do you have anything in your possession that you feel you should not have?

- Do you have anything in your possession which could injure yourself or others?

- Do you have any knives, needles or other sharp items in your possession?

If the answer to any of these questions is 'yes' you must not allow them to retrieve the item for you. Instead, you should ask them to keep their hands where you can see them before calling for the assistance of a colleague. Only retrieve the item in question when you are sure it is safe to do so.

3.7 Offensive weapons

Offensive weapons can take on a variety of descriptions and can even be something as insignificant and simple as a pencil. They can be disguised and hidden discreetly so you will need to be vigilant and thorough whilst conducting a search.

An offensive weapon can be defined as any object that has been made or adapted to cause injury. This covers anything from purpose-built weapons such as guns and knives, to a piece of wood that someone has

Activity: Search role play

Work in pairs, with one of you acting as a door supervisor and the other being a customer. Role play the procedures for conducting a manual search of customers entering the venue. The door supervisor must talk through their actions and complete a search register once the duty is complete.

picked up to swing at somebody. Section 1 of the Prevention of Crime Act 1953 makes it illegal to be in possession in a public place of an offensive weapon 'without lawful authority or reasonable excuse.'

Other examples of offensive weapons include:

- Bali song or butterfly knife
- Knuckleduster
- Telescopic truncheon
- Push dagger
- Shuriken or death star
- Hand claw
- Foot claw
- Manrikgusari or gusari
- Sword stick
- Hollow Kubatan
- Belt-buckle knife.

The majority of searches are uneventful. However, it is your professional duty and responsibility to safeguard yourself, your colleagues and all members of the public from offensive weapons.

3.8 Procedures for handling and recording articles seized during a search

Should you discover a prohibited item, you should ensure you record the following details:

- Date and time article seized
- How article was found
- Where the article was found
- Description of person it was found on or who it was found by (if handed in)
- Details of witnesses
- Description of item(s)
- Disposal of item (where stored)
- Action taken against person found with it in their possession
- Name of supervisor who was notified
- Name and number of police in attendance
- Signature of person making the entry.

Activity: Search procedures

1. What would you do if the customer was concealing a bottle of alcohol purchased elsewhere?
2. What would you do if the customer was concealing illegal substances such as drugs?
3. What would you do if the customer was concealing a weapon such as a knife?

If you are required to handle articles seized during a search you must make sure that you arrange an immediate handover of the articles to a supervisor or the police. Failing this you should ensure that you follow all of your venue's required internal procedures for storage or disposal of the articles.

4. Understand the powers of citizen's arrest and related procedures

4.1 Indictable offences

Arrestable offences are defined according to The Police and Criminal Evidence Act (PACE) 1984 and the Serious Organised Crime and Police Act (SOCPA) 2005 and include:

- Murder

- Rape and other sexual offences

- Assault (ABH, GBH and GBH with intent)

- Indecent assault

- Firearms offences

- Drugs offences

- Possession of offensive weapons

- Robbery

- Theft

- Burglary

- Deception

- Criminal damage.

These are different from summary offences which are relatively minor crimes dealt with in the Magistrates' Court.

4.2 What to consider before making a citizen's arrest

During your career you will encounter an enormous variety and diversity of situations. These will vary in seriousness and severity and no two will ever be the same. You may find yourself in situations where you will be witness to a variety of offences for which the apprehension of a suspect – an **arrest** – will need to made.

It is very important to remember that, as a door supervisor, your powers of arrest are the same as all members of the general public. You have

Key term

Arrest – to take away or deprive a person of their liberty

no legal advantage or special authority such as that of a police officer but you do have the legal right to apprehend individuals who are acting illegally.

A citizen's arrest must always be conducted within the strict confines of the law. It is essential that you become familiar with and knowledgeable about your rights, duties and responsibilities prior to, during and after making an arrest.

When you decide to arrest someone, you should not be doing so based on irrational judgement, speculation, hearsay, bias or prejudice. You will be equipped with sound judgement and the skills and professional expertise to ensure that you carry out the arrest procedure both within the law and with minimum conflict.

For a door supervisor to deprive an individual of his or her liberty – to arrest them – is a serious responsibility and, therefore, you will need to be aware of and follow set procedures to ensure the safety of those involved as well as yourself. You should consider what other options are available to you, the policy of your particular venue or premises, how a citizen's arrest might be perceived by the local police and the knock-on effect, such as being taken away from your primary duties and the inherent risk of violence involved in conducting a citizen's arrest.

Did you know?

The Human Rights Act 1998 Article 5 Section 1 states: Everyone has the right to liberty and security of person. No one shall be deprived of his liberty save in the following cases and in accordance with a procedure prescribed by law:

a) The lawful arrest or detention of a person after conviction by a competent court;

b) The lawful arrest or detention of a person for non-compliance with the lawful order of a court or in order to secure the fulfilment of any obligation prescribed by law;

c) The lawful arrest or detention of a person effective for the purpose of bringing him before the competent legal authority on reasonable suspicion of having committed an offence or when it is reasonably considered necessary to prevent his committing an offence or fleeing after having done so;

d) The detention of a minor by lawful order for the purpose of educational supervision or his lawful detention for the purpose of bringing him before the competent legal authority;

e) The lawful detention of persons for the prevention of the spreading of infectious diseases, of persons of unsound mind, alcoholics or drug addicts or vagrants; lawful order of a court or in order to secure the fulfilment of any obligation prescribed by law;

f) The lawful arrest or detention of a person to prevent his effecting an unauthorised entry into the country or of a person against whom action is being taken with a view to deportation or extradition.

4.3 Procedures for making a citizen's arrest

When you are certain that an arrestable offence has been committed and you know that you are acting lawfully, professionally and in the best interests of all concerned it will then be time for you to make an arrest.

You should not act over-aggressively or in a threatening manner as this is likely to result in a situation which could rapidly get out of control. You should act with assured confidence and restrained assertiveness to ensure that you remain in control of the procedure at all times. This will result in a successful outcome with the absolute minimum of physical contact and conflict.

The following procedure will safeguard both you and the suspect(s) who are involved in the arrest:

1. Begin by stating who you are – it may not always be obvious: **'I am an on-duty member of the security team…'**

2. Inform them that they are under arrest: **'and I am hereby arresting you…'**

3. State the offence: **'for the possession of an offensive weapon.'**

When you have successfully arrested the suspect it is your responsibility to detain him or her until the police arrive. This is also a very important part of the arrest procedure as you will be:

- ensuring the safe custody of the individual

- taking every precaution to prevent an escape

- maintaining the security of any items seized during the arrest

- preserving the evidence of a crime scene

- gathering evidence – witness statements

- recording all relevant information in a notebook/incident report.

It is highly unlikely that you will be in a situation where arrests will need to be made on a daily basis and it should only be made as a last resort.

By following the legal procedures when making an arrest and using your own skills, judgement, knowledge, intuition and overall professionalism you can be sure that you are acting not only in the best interests of all who are immediately concerned but also of the wider society.

4.4 Procedures after making a citizen's arrest

How you behave after the arrest of a citizen is every bit as important as how you conduct the arrest itself. There are four main considerations to be aware of.

1. **Ensuring the welfare of the person arrested.** You must ensure that the person you have detained is well treated and has access to basic facilities such as use of a toilet. You would not normally leave them unaccompanied. Remember, you are not part of the criminal justice system and you do not have their powers or their authority. If you mistreat a member of the public you could find yourself in court.

2. **Informing the police.** If you have conducted a citizen's arrest you must notify the police immediately and await their arrival.

3. **Detaining and supervising the suspect until the police arrive.** You must ensure that your arrestee is properly supervised while you are waiting for the police to arrive to ensure they do not commit further incidents or injure themselves. It is always better to have more than one person on supervision so that you have witnesses to any incidents that may arise and added protection for all parties.

4. **Incident report.** You should always complete your incident reports and paperwork as close to the time of the incident as possible so that your memory is fresh and your account of events is accurate. You may be called upon to relate your report in court or to the police so do not put it off.

5. Understanding relevant drug legislation and its relevance to the role of door supervisor

Drugs play a key role in almost every aspect of our everyday lives, from the common aspirin to the most advanced forms of medical treatment. Whilst the majority of drugs are freely available over the counter or by prescription there are a number that are illegal and it is your duty and responsibility as a professional door supervisor to act within the law to stop the entry of drugs into your venue.

5.1 Current drug legislation

The use of illegal substances is a common occurrence in many clubs, bars and entertainment venues. As a door supervisor your employer will expect you to prevent this activity by effective searches and be alert to drug offences that take place on the premises. The key piece of legislation you will be dealing with is the Misuse of Drugs Act 1971: under this act drugs are called 'controlled substances' and there are several main offences which you are likely to come across in the course of your work.

Possession

Possession is a crime under the Misuse of Drugs Act 1971. Possession is where a person has a controlled substance in their physical possession, such as in a pocket or handbag. The key categories under possession are:

- Possession – knowingly having a controlled substance about your person

- Joint possession – owning drugs with other people

- Past possession – where an attempt was made to destroy or dispose of the controlled substance, which was subsequently traced back to an individual.

Supply and use of premises

Supplying drugs to another person is an offence under the Misuse of Drugs Act. Supplying is seen as far more serious than possession and as you can see in Table 2DS.5 below carries a far harsher sentence. It is an offence to allow premises that you occupy or manage to be used for the purpose of drug taking or for the production or supply of controlled substances. This can have significant impact on entertainment venues and can even lead to them having their licence to operate permanently removed.

Controlled drugs classification system

Controlled substances are classified based on how harmful they are perceived to be (see Table 2DS.5 below). Class A drugs are the most harmful and Class C are less so.

Table 2DS.5: Examples of drugs from different classes and the associated punishments.

Class	Punishment	Substances
A	Possession: Up to 7 years and an unlimited fine. Supply: the maximum sentence is life imprisonment and an unlimited fine.	Ecstasy, LSD, Heroin, Cocaine, Crack Cocaine, Magic Mushrooms, Methadone, Meth Amphetamine (Crystal Meth), Any Class B drug, e.g. amphetamine, if prepared for injection.
B	Possession: Up to 5 years imprisonment and an unlimited fine. Supply: the maximum sentence is life imprisonment and an unlimited fine.	Amphetamines, Cannabis, Codeine (in strong concentration), Methylphenidate (Ritalin), Pholcodine
C	Possession: Up to two years imprisonment and an unlimited fine. Supply: the maximum sentence is 14 years and an unlimited fine.	Tranquilisers Some painkillers Gamma Hydroxbutyrate (GHB) Ketamine

Did you know?

Street names for controlled substances can have wide regional variations. It is important to check the slang names in your particular area of the country as they may be different to those listed on p.57.

5.2 and 5.3 Common indicators of drug misuse and common types of illegal drugs

In UK legislation you will see controlled substances referred to by their official names. However in the course of your duties as a door supervisor you are more like to hear them discussed by their various street names. Table 2DS.6 shows some of the most common controlled substances you may come across, their street names and their impact on the body and behaviour of the individual taking them.

Table 2DS.6: Physical and behavioural impacts of different drugs.

Controlled substance and street names	Physical impact	Behavioural impact
Ecstasy E, XTC, X, mitsubishis, dolphins	Raised body temperature, increased heart rate, tingling, increased energy. There have been over 200 Ecstasy-related deaths in the UK since 1996.	Talkative, affectionate, can lead to paranoia, anxiety and confusion. Not associated with violent behaviour.
Heroin H, Horse, Smack, Gear, Skag	Slows body functions, can cause dizziness and vomiting, highly addictive, HIV risk if shared needles are used, can cause respiratory failure.	Buzz or psychological rush, feeling of well being and relaxation, can cause sleepiness.
Cocaine Coke, charlie, C, snow, toot	Appetite suppressant, raised heartbeat, raised body temperature which can lead to convulsions and heart failure.	Feeling of being wide awake, confident, repeated use can cause loss of libido and panic attacks. Can cause depression.
Amphetamines Billy, whizz, speed, dexies	Can place a strain on the heart, puts the immune system under pressure leading to increased levels of general illness. Can be fatal in combination with alcohol or antidepressants, death from overdose is a risk factor.	Feeling of being wide awake, talkative, lots of energy, can dance for hours. Can be difficult to relax after a dose, and the 'come down' period can cause depression.
Cannabis Blow, pot, ganja, draw, weed, skunk, puff	Can cause nausea and vomiting, hunger pangs, increases the heart rate and can affect blood pressure, can trigger asthma attacks. Possible links to increased rates of mental illness.	Feeling of being relaxed and happy, talkative, giggly, sensory distortion such as time slowing, can cause anxiety and paranoia, tiredness and lack of concentration.
Gamma Hydroxybutrate Liquid ecstasy, GBH, GHB	Can cause unconsciousness, coma and death.	Creates feelings of euphoria, reduction of inhibitions and sleepiness, are a factor in some sexual assaults.
Ketamine K, Special K, Vitamin K	Reduces the functions of the nervous system, loss of physical sensation, can lead to unconsciousness.	Distortions in sensory perception, hallucinations, panic attacks and depression.

Physical evidence of drug use

Drug paraphernalia is a key give-away that drug use may have been occurring on your premises. Look for things such as:

- syringes and needles
- scorched tinfoil
- straws or rolled up bank notes/paper
- small pipes

- burnt spoons or cotton wool filters
- discarded paper wraps
- discarded cigarette ends with rolled cardboard filters.

Many, if not all, of the above items could be evidence from a crime scene, so location and time of discovery should always be entered into your notebook.

5.4 Signs of drug dealing

The effects of drug dealing and consumption can be catastrophic and even fatal. Individuals and groups in venues are subjected to loud music in a hot atmosphere. The effects of dehydration, exhaustion and drugs can lead to confusion, disorientation, collapse and unconsciousness.

It is your duty as a door supervisor to be aware of both drug dealing and drug taking and to act decisively in the first instance to prevent the drugs from entering the club or being used.

Targeting the drug dealer or dealers will be instrumental in preventing the spread of drugs throughout the venue and your patience and vigilance will be an invaluable asset to you and your team.

Many drug dealers tend to follow a certain pattern of behaviour that will help to identify them to potential customers; knowing and breaking these patterns can prevent the spread of drugs. Dealers will often place themselves in the same place each time they visit a venue and so there will be key areas where your surveillance skills will be important. You may also notice a number of apparently random individuals communicating with the same person for no particular reason. Another classic trait of a drug dealer is to continue surveying the area in the hope that they themselves are not being surveyed.

Once you feel you have identified a potential drug dealer, ask your fellow team members to assist you while you approach the individual, question, search and, if necessary, make an arrest.

5.5 Procedure for dealing with customers found in possession of drugs

There are, essentially, two ways of determining that an individual is in possession of drugs. This will be either during a general, random or specific search on entry or while on a routine check of the toilets or other area where you notice someone who appears to be distributing or taking drugs.

When confronted with such a situation, the following action must be taken:

A specific search on entry will determine if someone is in possession of drugs.

- Call for assistance but do not leave the area to seek help

- Search using the methods from your training

- Arrest and detain the person in possession of or supplying the drug

- Maintain observation of the arrested person(s) to prevent them hiding or swallowing the evidence

- Call the police

- Seize the drugs in the prescribed manner.

When the police arrive, explain what has happened and hand over all evidence using the correct procedures. If the police choose not to make an arrest or you decide not to call them, you would usually eject the person from the premises and ensure the safe and timely disposal of any controlled substances in conjunction with your local police service.

Then you should write a witness statement and incident report. When seizing drugs it is **essential** that the following details are recorded.

- Date and time article seized

- How article was found

- Where the article was found

- Description of person(s) it was found on

- Details of witnesses

- Description of item(s)

- Disposal of item (where stored)

- Action taken against person found with it in their possession

- Name of supervisor who was notified

- Name(s) and badge number(s) of police officer in attendance

- Signature of person making the entry.

By following these policies and procedures you will protect yourself, your team and your customers.

5.6 How to safely dispose of drug litter and waste

Drug litter and waste can be concealed in a variety of locations in a venue such as public toilets, in discarded litter (inside cigarette packets or drink cans), in bins, in alleyways and dark and concealed corners or spaces.

One of the biggest risks posed by drug litter is the potential for needle stick injuries. The risks include blood-borne diseases (e.g. hepatitis and HIV/AIDS). It is better to take the view that all needles found could be potentially infected, therefore the risk will need to be managed.

Did you know?

You need to be extremely careful when dealing with discarded needles and syringes as they pose a risk of disease.

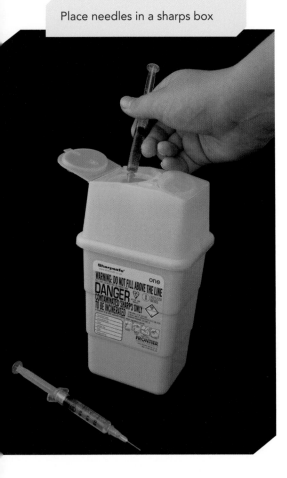

Place needles in a sharps box

When disposing of needles remember:

- Be alert! Look for obvious needles before handling waste or searching a person.

- Always wear suitable gloves. Gloves should not be relied on to give total protection, but they can help resist punctures in case of accidental contact.

- Sweep up needles with a dust pan and brush; or use a pincer tool.

- Do not try to re-sheath needles.

- Place needles in a sharps box – take the sharps box to the needle, not the needle to the sharps box (where possible). Try to put the sharps box on an even surface before opening it to deposit the needle.

- Never dispose of needles in the normal rubbish as this could injure someone else.

- You may need to hand needles to the police if they are evidence.

Remember to wear protective gloves when searching discreet areas such as the underside of a bar or behind a toilet facility, for example. Wear gloves when dealing with drug litter and contaminated waste (anything that is contaminated with bodily fluids). Flush any contaminated waste down the toilet. Drug awareness should also be adhered to when administering first aid so as to prevent the spread of infectious diseases.

6. Understanding incident recording and crime scene preservation

6.1 Types of records and reasons for a door supervisor to keep records

During the course of your work, you will be responsible for keeping various types of records such as a duty register, a pocket book and an incident book.

Duty register – a record of everyone working as security staff on a particular night. It should contain information such as:

- the registration number, name and address of a person

- the date and time at which he/she commenced duty with a signed acknowledgement by that person

- the date and time when he/she finished that period of duty with a signed acknowledgement by that person

- the name of the person or agency by whom that person is employed, if the person is not an employee of the licensee, or through whom the services of that person are engaged.

The register should be kept secure for a number of years and should be readily available if an authorised person or police officer wants to inspect it.

Pocket book – during the course of your work it will be necessary for you to keep detailed notes in your pocketbook. Such entries will need to include, for example, the times you start and finish, any incidents that have occurred, results of searches you have conducted and any health and safety issues.

Incident report – a log book of incidents should be kept by security staff at a venue. It should be kept up to date and should be completed as soon after an incident as possible to make sure it is accurate. It should record the following information:

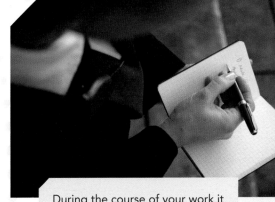

During the course of your work it will be necessary to keep detailed notes in your pocket book.

- Time of incident

- Manager on duty

- Staff involved

- Customers involved

- Witnesses

- Any police called and names and badge numbers

- Any door supervisor support called

- What happened

- Action taken

- Person deciding the action

- Incident details completed by (print name and sign).

It is important to keep the reporting of incidents factual, to the point and avoid writing anything that could be seen as offensive or personal.

Your records are an excellent way of keeping duty managers, bar staff and door supervisors up to date with anything that has happened since they last worked.

The information contained in your duty register, pocketbook and in any incident report forms could be vital evidence and may be used in court. It is essential that you record any accidents or incidents concisely and with as much detail as possible. The importance of accurate entries in your pocketbook and any subsequent incident reports cannot be overstated. What seems like a trivial event such as lost or found property may have serious consequences in the future and so every entry must be made with the same amount of diligence.

Records must be kept in a safe place and for a period of time. Records can be useful for you to reflect upon to improve procedure and policies, monitoring incidents that occur with any frequency or individuals who are consistently causing problems. Records can also be a way to protect yourself or the venue from false allegations as they provide valuable records of incidents, what happened and who was involved.

6.2 Incidents which need to be recorded and when the police are to be called

The following incidents need to be recorded:

- Any use of force
- Any first aid that has been administered
- Any accidents or near misses
- Any ejections that have occurred
- Any items found or seized during a search
- Any person who has been refused entry
- Anyone who is injured during an incident (staff or customer)
- Any fire incidents
- Any crimes that have been reported
- Any emergency calls made
- Any visits by statutory agencies or the police
- Customer complaints
- Lost or found property
- Any arrests
- Any customer disputes
- All other security-related incidents.

You should use your judgement as to whether the police should be called to attend an incident. You need to weigh up the seriousness of the incident, advice from management about calling the police and take into consideration any venue or local police policy.

6.3 Procedures for record keeping

As previously stated, an incident report and a pocketbook may contain vital information that can be used as evidence and it is therefore extremely important that the following guidelines are followed when making entries.

- Completed line by line, page by page.

The importance of making accurate entries in your pocketbook and any subsequent incident reports cannot be overstated.

- Pages should contain a margin on the left side for dates and times and be sequentially numbered.

- Spaces must not be left between entries and last line of text should be finished with a signature.

- Correction fluid should not be used; errors should be crossed through with a single line and initialled.

- Entries should only be made in ink.

- Pages should not be removed from the incident report or pocketbook.

- Never enter personal details into the pocketbook.

- Alarm, keypad or computer log-in codes should not be recorded in the incident report or pocketbook.

The more information you can record the more it could assist in a successful police investigation or help you to review the venue's policies, staffing levels and risk management. An incident report should, as a minimum, contain covering information about you and the context, a detailed description of the incident itself, who was involved, details of any witnesses who could verify the report and what action you and your colleagues took to resolve the situation.

6.4 Different types of evidence

Crime scenes can vary considerably and may involve fire, drugs, violence or negligence. However, they will all have several aspects in common with regard to the different types of evidence, which are outlined in Table 2DS.7 below.

Table 2DS.7: Descriptions of different types of evidence

Type of evidence	Description
Direct evidence	Something that has been seen, heard or experienced by an individual and it is that individual who relates it firsthand; either as a witness at the scene or later in court. An example of direct evidence would be an incident caught on CCTV camera.
Circumstantial evidence	Evidence that does not necessarily prove outright that the offence was committed by a certain person but it does suggest a link. When combined with other types of evidence it can, nonetheless, be compelling. For example, a person may report that their purse has been stolen and another customer is seen using the purse. There are no witnesses who saw the person taking the purse (direct evidence) but the fact that the person is in possession of a stolen article (circumstantial evidence) could be seen as compelling evidence that they may have committed an offence.
Documentary evidence	Evidence which is usually presented as a written document, such as an incident report, a witness statement or a door supervisor's pocketbook. In this regard, the information you record is extremely important.
Expert evidence	Evidence provided by an expert. This could be, for example, a fire scene investigator who is a specialist in his or her field, or a medical expert. Once again, the evidence you initially provide could be critical in that investigation.

Table 2DS.7 (cont.)

Type of evidence	Description
Corroborating evidence	Occasionally, the information given by a single witness may be lacking in clarity or detail and may therefore be regarded as insubstantial. If, however, it is used in conjunction with similar types of evidence such as that provided by another witness, it gains strength and is, therefore, of particular importance.
Real evidence	Evidence which can be physically presented in court, such as a knife, screwdriver, drugs or stolen goods.
Forensic evidence	Evidence which usually requires expert input, such as DNA evidence from blood and hair, fingerprint analysis, ballistics or evidence gleaned from footprints or car tyres. Although it is mainly circumstantial, forensic evidence can be crucial corroborating evidence in court.
Hearsay	This is something which a person has not witnessed themselves but has heard from others. As a general rule, hearsay evidence is not admissible evidence in court.

6.5 Rules that need to be followed to preserve evidence and crime scenes

As you will be primarily responsible for preserving evidence at a crime scene it is necessary that you take every precaution to avoid contamination. You must, therefore, prevent any persons from:

- entering the scene and adding fingerprints, footprints or leaving traces of hair and saliva

- entering the scene and tidying up the area

- entering the area and disturbing, removing, or destroying items, which could contain valuable evidence

- entering the scene and moving bodies

- using the scene as a thoroughfare.

You must also provide adequate warning to those within the area not to touch, disturb or interfere with the crime scene.

The easiest way of preserving evidence at a crime scene is to cordon it off quickly and efficiently. If the crime scene is outside you may need to improvise by using anything at hand (jackets, bricks or even people placed at strategic points to minimise entrance). Ideally, though, you should use tape which can be secured around lamp posts, traffic lights, car wing mirrors or garden fence posts. Depending on the location of the crime scene the following should be noted when cordoning off an area:

- Use tape or a suitable alternative to seal off the scene and surrounding areas.

- Block off or lock access points (considering Health and Safety).

- Close windows.

- Cover exposed evidence such as footprints to prevent contamination.

- Restrict access to and from the scene.

- Guard the area at all times.

You should only allow authorised personnel to enter a crime scene and these should include:

- detective officers

- photographers

- fingerprint officers

- dog handlers

- supervisory officers

- paramedics doctors or first aid trained staff

- fire service personnel if arson is suspected

- accident investigators.

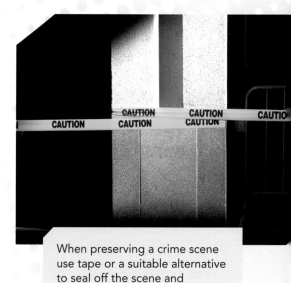

When preserving a crime scene use tape or a suitable alternative to seal off the scene and surrounding areas.

7. Understanding licensing law and social responsibility relating to licensed premises

When you work as security on the doors of a licensed venue you will be responsible for handling situations where alcohol plays a major part in people's behaviour. This may involve mediating in an argument in order to defuse the situation, escorting an intoxicated person from the premises or calling the emergency services for assistance. It is therefore important that you are aware of the current licensing laws and how to apply them in your everyday life.

7.1 Licensing objectives under current alcohol licensing legislation

The **Licensing Act of 2003** is an Act that applies only to England and Wales. A single licence is granted to premises which are used for the sale or supply of alcohol and may also include providing entertainment or late-night refreshments. Responsibility for issuing licences rests with local authorities.

The Act sets out four licensing objectives. They are:

- the prevention of crime and disorder
- public safety
- prevention of public nuisance
- the protection of children from harm.

7.2 Different types of licences issued and activities they allow

There are various types of licence which allow different types of activities on the premises (see Table 2DS.8).

Table 2DS.8: Types of licence

Type of licence	Description
Personal licence	This licence authorises individuals to sell or supply alcohol, or authorise the sale and supply of alcohol, for consumption on or off the premises. A personal licence is issued for 10 years in the first instance. The licence is 'portable' and will allow the licence holder to work in any premises in England or Wales holding a valid premises licence, which permits the supply of alcohol.
Premises licence	This licence authorises the holder of the licence to a premises for licensable activities. The supply of alcohol under a premises licence must be made by or under the authority of a personal licence holder – designated premises supervisor. The licence shows in detail the operating conditions such as hours of trading, duration of the licence, who is to act as the designated premises supervisor and how the licensing objectives will be promoted. There is no time limit to a premises licence unless it is revoked or surrendered.
Club premises certificate	This applies to members' clubs and is similar to a premises licence. The main difference is that there is no need for a designated premises supervisor. This will be covered by the club's management committee.
Temporary event notice	A temporary event notice is required if you intend to carry out a licensable activity on unlicensed premises or wish to operate outside the terms of an existing premises licence or club premises licence. This type of licence is designed for small-scale one-off events, or situations where premises licences do not meet the needs of a particular function on a particular night; for example somebody may want a special birthday party at a later time than is included on the premises licence, or it may be held in a marquee in a garden of a pub which is not covered under the premises licence. The maximum number of people who can enjoy the licensable activities is 499 including staff and any performers.

Personal licences, premises licences and club premises certificates are granted by licensing authorities that are usually in the local authority for the area in which a premises is located.

7.3 Circumstances under which customers can be ejected

There are circumstances in which a customer can be ejected and you should be aware of what these are. In general, an individual can be ejected from a premises for breaches of conditions of entry, for breaking the law or for unacceptable behaviour.

If a person is under age or if your venue has strict dress codes you may refuse entry or ask a person to leave the premises.

If you suspect that an individual is drunk – they are incapable of rational thought and behaviour, find it difficult to communicate, or are aggressive for no apparent reason – then you have the right to refuse entry or eject them from the premises. However, if the situation escalates and the individual becomes drunk and **disorderly** on licensed premises then you have the power of arrest, although this should only apply as a last resort.

Under the Licensing Act 1964, licensees and their agents also have a legal duty in respect of people being or found to be drunk on licensed premises. It is an offence to allow drunkenness or violent, quarrelsome or riotous conduct to take place on licensed premises. It is also an offence to sell alcohol to anyone who is deemed to be drunk, or for anyone else to buy or attempt to buy alcohol for someone who is drunk. The police may be called upon to help eject anyone refusing to leave a licensed premises.

If a customer is breaking the law – such as taking or supplying drugs or involved in prostitution – you should ask them to leave the venue and in some cases contact the police.

A customer may be abusive, violent or sexually harassing other customers. Unacceptable behaviour such as this also warrants removing a customer from a venue.

7.4 Police powers with regard to licensed premises

Due to the nature of your job you will frequently find yourself working alongside the police and it is therefore important that you are aware of their powers and position in similar circumstances. The police may:

- enter licensed premises without a warrant during permitted hours and drinking-up times in order to prevent or detect licensing offences

- enter licensed premises without a warrant outside permitted hours if they have reasonable grounds to suspect a licensing offence is being or about to be committed

- enter premises and conduct a search if they believe that drug offenses or breaches of the peace have occurred

- close a premises if it is too noisy, in danger of threatening public safety or disorderly.

If you suspect a person is under age you may refuse entry or ask a person to leave the premises.

It is also necessary for you to observe the following:

- It is an offence for a member of staff or a door supervisor to refuse entry to the police.

- A licensee cannot allow an on-duty police officer to remain unnecessarily on the premises except in the execution of their duties.

- A licensee cannot serve an on-duty police officer intoxicating liquor without prior authority of the police officer's superior.

7.5 The power of entry of authorised persons

If an authorised person (for example from the Licensing Authority or from the Weights and Measures Authority) has reason to believe that there is any breach of a licence, they are able to enter the premises with a view to seeing if activity is being carried out in accordance with a licence. Obstructing an authorised person intentionally is an offence.

7.6 The rights and duties of the licensees and door supervisors and their representatives

The licensee, the holder of the licence of a venue, is responsible and therefore liable for any lawful misconduct committed by his or her employees – even if he or she is not present when an offence is committed.

The licence holder can also be convicted of an offence even if the employee has acted with total disregard to the express instructions of the licence holder. As a door supervisor you will be acting as an agent for the licence holder and, as such, you will be held responsible for both the observance and breach of licensing laws. The responsibilities of a door supervisor include right to refuse entry, to withdraw consent to be on a premises, to eject customers from a premises for reasons stated above, and to prevent breaches of licensing laws and other illegal activity.

7.7 Legislation regarding children and young people

You may well find someone who you suspect is under the legal age to consume alcohol on licensed premises. Your aim, duty and responsibility is to stop this from happening. Therefore, you should be aware of the law and its exemptions so the following must be observed.

Normally persons under the age of 18 years old cannot:

- buy alcohol on licensed premises

- consume alcohol on licensed premises.

Exemptions from this are:

- Persons aged 16 years or over may be allowed to drink beer, porter, cider or perry (not normal wine) with a meal in a part of the venue set aside for table meals. They may also purchase the same within the designated area.

- A person under 14 years of age is not permitted in the bar of licensed premises during permitted hours. Exemptions to this are:

  o A children's certificate is in force

  o The person is a child of the licensee

  o The child lives on the premises

  o The child is walking through the bar to get elsewhere and there is no other route to follow.

If you suspect that an individual is under age and they do not fall into any of the previous categories then you will need to ask for proof of age. It is the responsibility of that individual to prove to your satisfaction that they are of the legal age and the following list shows what is classed as acceptable proof:

- Military ID (MOD form 90 etc)

- Passport

- Picture driving licence

- Student union picture ID

- National Proof of Age scheme card

- Any other approved identification.

If you suspect that an individual is under age then you will need to ask for proof of age.

7.8 Activities considered unlawful under licensing, gaming and sexual offences legislation

Alcohol-related incidents and, indeed, accidents are not the only areas where you will need to be aware of certain laws and how to apply and uphold them: activities such as prostitution and gambling are also unlawful under licensing legislation. The Licensing Act of 1964 states that:

'Prostitutes are not to be allowed to assemble on licensed premises or the premises to be used as a brothel.'

Gaming machines will need an operating licence from the Gaming Commission

Did you know?

Gaming machines are categorised according to how much it costs to play a game and the maximum prize money that a game can pay out.

The Act goes on to say:

'The holder of a licence shall not knowingly allow the licensed premises to be the habitual resort or place of meeting of reputed prostitutes, whether the object of their so resorting or meeting is or is not prostitution; but this section does not prohibit his allowing any such persons to remain in the premises for the purpose of obtaining reasonable refreshment for such time as is necessary for that purpose.'

Likewise the following Gaming Laws should be enforced. The Licensing Act 1964 states:

'The licensee shall not allow any game to be played on the premises in such circumstances that an offence under the Gaming Act 1968 is committed.'

However, the following exemptions apply:

• The premises is licensed for such gaming

• Games of pure skill such as snooker and darts may be played and players may place stakes on the outcome of the game

• Games of combined skill and chance, such as cribbage and dominoes are permitted by the licensing justices – who will impose conditions within the specific licence

• Coin-operated gaming machines may be played if the appropriate licences have been obtained and are in force.

Gaming machines, commonly known as fruit machines, will need an operating licence from the Gambling Commission and a premises licence from the Licensing Authority.

Games are categorised according to the minimum that can be paid for playing the machine and the maximum prize that someone can win (see Table 2DS.9 below). There is a minimum age of 18 for all players for all category A, B and C machines. For a category C game the minimum amount to play the game is 50p and the maximum prize money is £35. However category C machines must be in a separate area to ensure the segregation and supervision of machines that may only be played by adults.

Table 2DS.9: Maximum stake and minimum prize of different categories of gaming machine

Category of machine	Maximum stake	Minimum prize
A	Unlimited	Unlimited
B1	£2	£4000
B2	£100 (in multiples of £10)	£500
B3A	£1	£500
B3	£1	£500
B4	£1	£250
C	50p	£35
D	10p	£5
	30p	£8

It is important to observe and uphold the legislation concerning the licensing laws to safeguard yourself, your colleagues and your customers. Failure to do so could result in a premises losing its licence and fines being imposed.

8. Understanding safety and security issues relevant to door supervisors

As a door supervisor it is inevitable that you will be required to deal with safety and security issues on a regular basis. Understanding the key issues will help you perform better in your role.

8.1 Understand common human responses in an emergency situation

Emergencies such as first aid incidents, evacuations and security alerts can all trigger various responses in staff and customers. The most common ones are:

- Reluctance to accept emergency is happening – On a night out people may be more relaxed and less alert than usual, alcohol may have slowed their responses and they may not see an emergency develop or respond quickly when they do realise a situation exists. People can be reluctant to acknowledge they may need to leave a venue quickly or clear the area to allow emergency crews to respond. This makes it extremely important that, as a door supervisor, you are vigilant and responsive to developing situations.

- Calmness – People in emergency situations can become very calm, sometimes as a response to shock.

- Increased cooperation and altruistic behaviour – You may see people working together to clear the area or rescue people left behind in a dangerous situation.

- Fear and distress – One of the most common responses is fear and distress. This can be dangerous as it may cause panic and stampedes for the exit. This can cost more lives in the long run as people can be trampled in the panic.

It is better to limit the number of people in a venue to ensure that people can be easily and safely evacuated in case of an emergency

8.2 Reasons for having fire risk assessments and maximum occupancy figures

All entertainment venues are required to have a fire risk assessment and a maximum occupancy figure. Clubs and pubs can be very crowded, and a fire in a venue at full capacity could have disastrous consequences. The purpose of a fire risk assessment is primarily to reduce the hazards which may contribute to a fire beginning in the first place and put control measures in place to ensure that any remaining hazards are minimised.

An overcrowded venue with little room to manoeuvre can create crushes where people can be injured; this is even more apparent when people have to exit the premises quickly in case of a fire. It is better to limit the capacity and keep people inside the venue safe and be able to evacuate quickly than to have a packed venue where people could be seriously hurt.

Case study: E2 Nightclub

In 2003 21 people died and 50 were injured in a stampede at the E2 nightclub in Chicago. A fight had broken out in the club and the security team had attempted to break up the fight using pepper spray. This caused vomiting and fainting in some clubbers, leading to panic and a rush for the exit as people suspected a terrorist attack. The main exit was down a deep stairwell and the doors opened inwards. People who had been entering the club using the stairwell were knocked down and pinned in the crush of 1500 people trying to escape the club at the same time. In 2009, the owners of the club were acquitted of manslaughter but sentenced to two years' imprisonment for indirect criminal contempt as the nightclub was under orders to close at the time of the incident.

Over to you

1. What factor might overcrowding have played in this incident?
2. How could a fire and evacuation risk assessment have controlled this situation?
3. What is your view on the role of the club security in this incident?

8.3 Behaviours that could indicate unusual and suspicious activities

A door supervisor should always be alert for actions which could indicate something out of the ordinary is happening. Since entertainment venues are often high-profile premises in communities and contain hundreds of people in a relatively small area they can become targets for criminal activity.

There are key things you should be aware of:

- Surveillance – Is your premises under surveillance? Are people watching for shift changes, security checks or testing the range of the CCTV? It may be that they are looking for an area which could be used for drug dealing without being observed or using unmonitored space for criminal activities.

- Questioning about the premises – Is there a customer who seems unusually interested in your premises? Are they asking about entrances and exits, numbers of staff, club capacity, etc? They could be gathering information in order to commit criminal activity.

- Tests of security – Have the emergency exits been opened by accident? Have customers tried to get into secure areas and claimed they didn't know where they were going? Criminals will often test security before they commit a crime to see how responsive security staff are and how easy the target is to infiltrate. On a busy night, clubs will have thousands of pounds in cash on the premises, making them a profitable target if security is slow or lax.

- People, objects and behaviour that are out of place – You should always keep an eye out for people, objects and behaviour that are out of place as an indicator that something needs additional investigation. Being alert like this can prevent injury, crime and theft on your premises.

8.4 Current terrorism issues and procedures

The threat of terrorism is not often associated with an entertainment environment, but there have been terrorist attacks on nightclub venues across the world. The most serious of these incidents were the 2002 Bali bombings which killed 202 people and injured a further 240. In 2007 a car packed with petrol, nails and gas was left outside the Tiger Tiger nightclub in London. Security staff in entertainment venues should be vigilant at all times.

There are some key actions that can help prevent terrorist activities against your premises. Ensure that you are vigilant for individuals who are watching your premises as they may be engaged in hostile reconnaissance: searching for weaknesses in your security arrangements or search patterns. It is important to be especially vigilant for suspect packages and cars, even if they turn out to be harmless, as they could be a 'dry run' for the real thing. Maintaining a visible presence will also help deter and disrupt possible terrorist activity as will your routine searching of premises and screening of your customers. It is very important to report and record all incidents as they could be connected with other incidents elsewhere and provide a clearer picture for the government security agencies to work from.

8.5 Common situations requiring first aid

As a door supervisor you should ensure you have a current first aid certificate and your premises has sufficient equipment and resources to allow you to administer first aid until an ambulance crew arrives. Some of the most common first aid situations you will find in a typical entertainment venue are included in Table 2DS.10 below.

Table 2DS.10: Cause of first aid situations.

Cause of first aid situation	Description
Accidents (slips, trips and falls)	Combinations of things such as high heels, alcohol, stairs, mirrored walls and reduced lighting can cause trips, slips and falls in your venue. Your risk assessments should indicate where the key risk areas are and address them with control measures such as better lighting in areas with stairs, or warning signs. As a first aider you could deal with injuries from sprained ankles and wrists to broken bones and concussion.
Violence	The mixture of alcohol and an enclosed environment can cause conflict in pubs and clubs. Common first aid situations resulting from violence can be cuts and bruises to the face and body, injury to the nose, mouth and eyes and in extreme cases where a weapon has been used there could be serious knife or gunshot wounds.
Drug overdose	Most entertainment venues understand that they risk losing their licence and being closed down if they do not tackle drug use on their premises. However, a determined customer will find a way to get drugs past security. This can lead to drug overdoses in your venue and you must be ready to provide emergency aid and call for the paramedic team.
Epilepsy	You may have to deal with pre-existing medical conditions such as epilepsy while you are on duty. It can be very difficult to distinguish between drunken behaviour and symptoms such as disorientation, confusion and drowsiness which can be a side effect of an epileptic seizure.

Case study: Daniel Chapman

In 2008 Daniel Chapman and his wife Clair were enjoying a night out with friends at Liquid nightclub in Hanley. After suffering a seizure at the club Mr Chapman became disorientated, confused and aggressive resulting in him being ejected from the club by the security staff. He was taken to hospital by ambulance after suffering a total of five fits. Members of Mr Chapman's party claim they tried to tell the door staff that they were dealing with an episode of epilepsy, but he was physically ejected from the club anyway. The club manager noted that it was extremely difficult for even first aid trained door staff to tell the difference between customers who

are violent and dangerous as a result of alcohol and those who may be suffering other conditions, but that the safety of the other customers in the vicinity is the first priority of the door staff.

Over to you

1. As a door supervisor how would you have dealt with the above situation?

2. How important is first aid training to the work of a good door supervisor?

3. How do you balance the needs of the casualty with the safety needs of other customers?

8.6 How to safely dispose of contaminated waste

Your first aid training should include the use of gloves when dealing with casualties and how to deal with the associated waste. Contamination can be through blood, saliva or other bodily fluids. You should always avoid direct skin contact with contaminated waste as some diseases and infections can be transmitted through bodily fluids. This means you should wear surgical gloves, ensure your premises has a sharps disposal box for needles and syringes, and disposal bags for wound dressings, bandages and cotton wool. All staff involved in dealing with first aid incidents should understand the importance of thorough hand washing with antibacterial soap to remove traces of contamination and to prevent the spread of infection.

Just checking

1. Describe three different types of assault.

2. Why is it important to have an admissions policy to a venue?

3. Which illegal drugs are you most likely to come into contact with at an entertainment venue?

4. What are the common street names for cocaine, heroin and amphetamines?

5. List five key qualities of a door supervisor.

6. Why does a door supervisor need to demonstrate high standards of behaviour?

7. What types of property offences are you likely to have to deal with as a door supervisor?

8. Why would you conduct a premises search?

9. What is an indictable offence?

10. How would you make a citizen's arrest?

11. Which drugs legislation relates to your role as a door supervisor?

12. Under what circumstances might customers be ejected from a venue?

13. What are the common responses to an emergency?

14. Why are clubs required to have a maximum occupancy figure?

15. What common situations might require a first aid response in licensed premises?

Obasi Akani
Door supervisor

I got into working in door supervision for a friend of mine who I practised martial arts with. The venue where my friend worked was short of staff and my friend suggested me. I did a four-day door supervisor course and worked part-time at the same time as working my day job. I have been a door supervisor for over five years now and I really enjoy the experience.

I have found that there is a lot of camaraderie between the staff working at the venue and I have made a lot of friends doing this job. It helps if you do work well with your colleagues as you tend to work better as a team.

I also like the fact that I get to work with a lot of customers from a range of different backgrounds. We get our regulars who we build up a good rapport with.

I also like being able to deal with a range of different conflict situations. It makes me feel really pleased when I have been able to defuse a potentially explosive situation just by talking to people.

Over to you

1. Reflect on what you have learnt in this unit.
2. What aspects of the job do you think you will like?
3. What things do you think will be a challenge?
4. Do you think there are personal and physical attributes that make a good door supervisor?

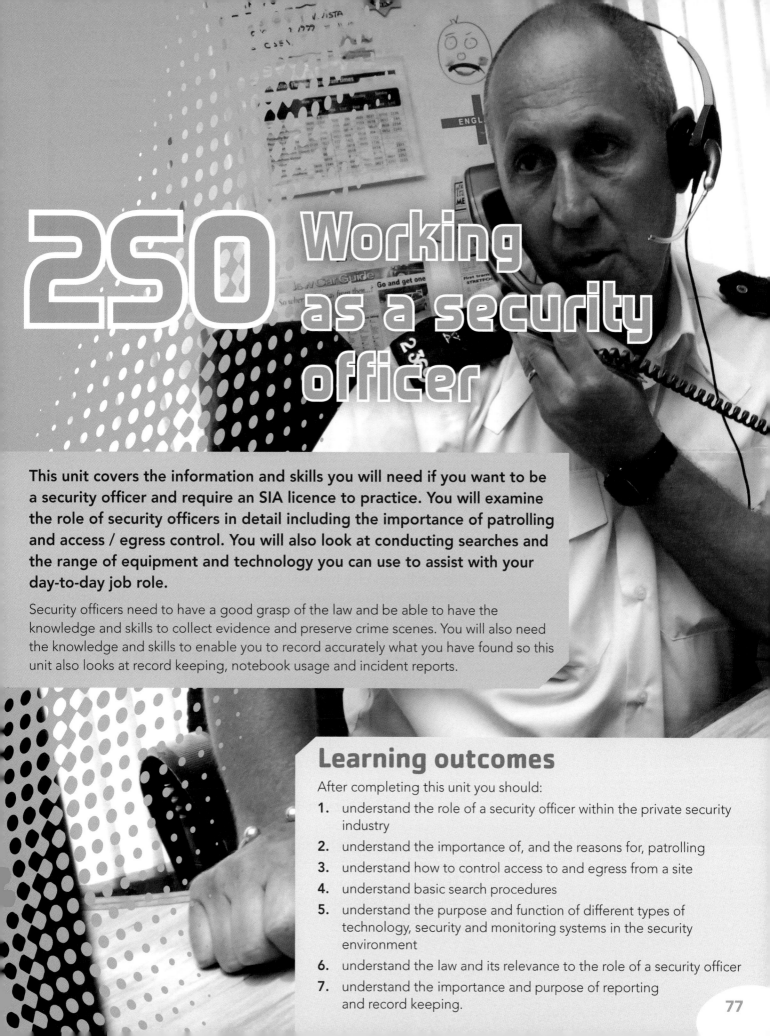

250 Working as a security officer

This unit covers the information and skills you will need if you want to be a security officer and require an SIA licence to practice. You will examine the role of security officers in detail including the importance of patrolling and access / egress control. You will also look at conducting searches and the range of equipment and technology you can use to assist with your day-to-day job role.

Security officers need to have a good grasp of the law and be able to have the knowledge and skills to collect evidence and preserve crime scenes. You will also need the knowledge and skills to enable you to record accurately what you have found so this unit also looks at record keeping, notebook usage and incident reports.

Learning outcomes

After completing this unit you should:

1. understand the role of a security officer within the private security industry
2. understand the importance of, and the reasons for, patrolling
3. understand how to control access to and egress from a site
4. understand basic search procedures
5. understand the purpose and function of different types of technology, security and monitoring systems in the security environment
6. understand the law and its relevance to the role of a security officer
7. understand the importance and purpose of reporting and record keeping.

Security alert!

Being a security officer

There are lots of opportunities to work in different sectors of the security industry such as:

- the commercial sector
- the public sector
- personal security
- transportation of vehicles
- entertainment security.

What do you think are the advantages and disadvantages of each sector? Draw up a list of pros and cons for each one. Which sector has the most advantages for you to work in?

1. Understand the role of a security officer within the private security industry

If you are going to work as a security officer in the private security industry then it is important that you understand some of their key responsibilities. The British Security Industry Association (BSIA) estimates that its members employ over 75,500 security officers in the UK and its companies have an annual combined turnover of £1.6 billion. So you will be joining a vibrant and growing sector.

1.1 Responsibilities of a security officer

Although security officers can work in a variety of settings such as entertainment venues, shopping centres, businesses and the public sector, their main duties and responsibilities are largely the same wherever they are.

- **Prevention and detection of crime and unauthorised activities.**
  This involves protecting individuals and premises from criminal activities such as theft, criminal damage and arson. It also involves preserving any evidence found at the scene of a crime until the police arrive. Security officers also have a responsibility to prevent any unauthorised activities which their employer or client wishes to forbid on their premises, such as drinking alcohol or personal use of equipment.

- **Prevention and reduction of loss, waste and damage.** Prevention of loss is a key responsibility. In large companies it can be easy for stock to be misplaced or stolen due to the size of the premises, number of deliveries and volume of people passing through. Effective security can reduce this loss and limit waste and damage.

- **Monitoring and responding to safety risks.** A key responsibility of an effective security officer is to identify risks and respond to them. This includes reporting security issues such as broken windows and locks which may allow thieves to access premises, and ensuring the public are not exposed to risk on the premises.

- **Responsibilities in emergencies.** Emergency situations can and do happen and security personnel must be clear about their responsibilities, which can include evacuation, first aid, liaising with the emergency services and securing premises.

- **Control of access and egress.** This is the responsibility for managing entry to (access) and exit (egress) from premises. It is important to control who enters so that you know who is on the premises and why, and so the premises don't become overcrowded. It is also important to monitor when they leave so you can be sure who is on the premises at a given time for safety purposes.

One of the roles of a security guard is to manage entry to and exit from the premises.

1.2 Purposes of assignment instructions

Assignment instructions are provided to a security officer to meet the needs of their client. They give clear instructions for the officer to follow when they are carrying out their duties on site.

Table 2SO.1: Purpose of assignment instructions

Purpose	Explanation and / or examples
Provide information and procedures	Specific instructions on what to do and how to do it. It acts as a clear source of information for the guard on how that particular client wants the job done.
Aid to meet the needs of the client	Clients usually add to or amend the assignment instructions to suit their needs or benefit their business, so the security officer can better meet their needs. Assignment instructions are usually signed off by the client, so they are fully aware of how security will operate at their site.
Outline typical tasks and provide supporting information	May contain specific instructions on patrolling, control of access and egress or any other duties, as well as risk assessment information and emergency procedures. They are a working document and should be referred to on a daily basis by security personnel.

1.3 Items of equipment needed

Part of your responsibility as a security officer is to ensure you have the right equipment with you in order to conduct your job safely and professionally. Generally there are two forms of equipment you might need:

- **Health and safety equipment.** Uniform, personal protective equipment (PPE) in the form of boots, duty belts, mini-first aid kits, torch, protective vests, or more specialised equipment such as helmets depending on the type of premises being secured, for example security personnel for cash in transit might be issued with body armour.

- **Patrolling equipment.** A strong and durable torch, such as a six-cell Maglite®, identification card or badge, a means of communication such as radio or phone, high-visibility jacket, patrol tour system if the premises has one, logbook and pen.

A high-visibility jacket can be worn when patrolling.

Case study: Tour patrol systems

Sam is a security officer for a large multi-national computer company in the East Midlands. He works with a team of staff who each have their own designated patrol areas around the site.

"We have recently had a patrol tour system installed at the premises where I work, specifically for the night shift. We operate on a 24-hour basis at this site, but the duties during business hours and off hours are slightly different. During the day we control access to and exit from the premises, check identification, oversee the car park and respond to on-premises incidents. However in the evening and at night the role becomes more about securing the premises and patrolling to ensure the buildings and equipment are safe. The tour patrol system works by logging our patrol routes and times. As I do my patrol there are control points on the wall with sensors and I hold up my ID tag and it registers I've checked that area. It means my supervisor can download the information and see if we have done our patrols on time and secured all the areas given to us in our assignment instructions."

Over to you

1. What benefits might a tour patrol system have for a security company?

2. What benefits might a tour patrol system have for the business client?

3. What is the impact on security officers of using a system like this?

1.4 Confidentiality within the role of a security officer

Confidentiality is a key part of the role of a security officer. You will come into contact with confidential information on a daily basis and your employer and their client must be able to trust that you will not share the information with others who are not authorised to have it and who may use the information to hurt your company or customers.

Confidentiality about procedures, systems, alarm codes and access codes

During the course of your work you will know alarm codes, access codes, possible weaknesses in the security of premises and patrol routes and times. All of this information could leave a company vulnerable to attack if it were known to the public. Part of your role is to ensure you do not share this information with anyone who does not need to have access to it.

Confidentiality of data and records

In some premises where security operates you will have access to confidential records or data, such as medical records, names and addresses of clients, plans, blueprints, business proposals, payroll and criminal record checks. You need to uphold the highest standards of professionalism if you come across confidential information.

Who does confidentiality apply to?

Confidentiality applies to all employees of an organisation or those under subcontract to provide services such as security. Generally there will be a confidentiality clause in your contract or you will be required to sign a separate confidentiality agreement to ensure you understand your responsibilities.

Repercussions of breaching confidentiality

If you breach confidentiality in the workplace you will face severe consequences. Firstly your employer could decide to dismiss you for gross misconduct; you could therefore lose your job and your income. Secondly you may face civil charges if a company decides to pursue you through the courts so you may also end up in a costly legal battle. It would also be very unlikely you would find work in the security field again if you cannot be trusted.

Whistleblowing

Whistleblowing is when an employee provides information that has come to their attention during the course of their work to the authorities. It is the process of releasing confidential information in the interests of the public. The key piece of legislation covering whistleblowing is the Public Interest Disclosure Act 1998 which protects people who release information if they do so to an appropriate body

> ### Key term
>
> **Confidentiality** – ensuring that information remains only with those who are authorised to have access to it.

> ### Activity: Whistleblowing
>
> In which of the following situations might it be appropriate to breach confidentiality and become a whistleblower?
>
> 1. You are conducting evening patrols and come across a computer in an office, which has highly indecent materials displayed on it.
> 2. You come across documents which indicate that patients are being given incorrect medication in a hospital.
> 3. You are unhappy with the quality of your PPE.
> 4. A colleague allows his brother to have your company's client list as he is setting up his own business and needs contacts.

such as the HSE or the senior management of the company and it relates to some sort of danger or illegal behaviour which could affect others.

During the course of your work you will have access to alarm codes and access codes. Why is it important that you do not pass on these details?

1.5 Purposes of control rooms

A control room is the hub of a successful security operation and deals with a variety of tasks (see Table 2SO.2 below).

Table 2SO.2: Control room activity

Control room activity	Description
Monitoring and logging of local staff activity	A control room will monitor the work patterns and duties of security personnel to ensure they are conducted appropriately. This may include specially designed monitoring systems such as tour patrol systems or other methods.
Coordination of radio and communications	Control rooms act as the central hub for communications. They contact officers who are lone working to ensure their safety, ensure important information is passed to the appropriate staff and provide regular situation updates as required.
Monitoring of CCTV and alarm systems	Many control rooms also have a bank of monitors where CCTV can be monitored and incident information relayed to security personnel at the scene. Security companies also offer 24-hour alarm monitoring systems for premises so that if an alarm is triggered it automatically flags up in the control room and a security officer can be sent to respond.
Providing additional support when required	The control room also coordinates support for officers at premises, including calling the emergency services, sending additional security personnel out and liaising between officers at different sites.

2. Understand the importance of, and the reasons for, patrolling

Patrolling is a key role of a security officer. It can be done on foot or in a vehicle, solo or as part of a team. This part of the course looks at the types of patrol you might need to do and the planning and equipment that you will need in order to patrol effectively.

2.1 Types and purposes of patrols

Unlock or takeover patrol – This is where you might be required to open a site for business; this includes unlocking access points so employees can enter, ensuring car park barriers are operational or staffed and ensuring the site is secured for the coming day's business. Depending on the size and type of premises this might be done alone, as part of a team or as part of the handover procedure from the security staff on night duty.

Routine patrol – This is the main aspect of patrolling for many security officers. It involves following assignment instructions for the shift which will outline an officer's planned monitoring, either via CCTV or in person, ensuring security is maintained across their area of responsibility and preventing and detecting criminal and unauthorised activities.

High-risk area patrol – Some of your clients may have areas that are at particular risk of criminal or unauthorised activities and a high-risk patrol focuses on those areas. It includes the same duties as a routine patrol, but at increased levels.

Lockup or handover patrol – This type of patrol involves securing the site after the day's business has concluded, making sure the premises are cleared of staff and alarm systems are initiated. Depending on the type of business it may also involve handing over responsibility to the night duty officers.

2.2 Actions before starting a patrol

The key to patrolling is effective planning and preparation. A patrol is not just a stroll round a site while you keep your eyes open for problems. It is a much more focused and professional activity.

In order to ensure your patrol is effective you should consider the following actions:

Checks of instructions, records and logs

- Have you checked your assignment instructions?
- If you are taking over from another officer/shift, did you check their records?
- Have you checked the day's logs?
- Do you have your logbook?
- Have you spoken with your supervisor?
- Do you know your patrol route?

Checks of patrol equipment

- Are you wearing your PPE?
- Is your PPE in good condition?
- Do you have your ID fob if you are linked to a tour patrol system?
- Do you need a torch?
- Do you have your radio?
- Do you need high-visibility clothing?
- Are you equipped for poor weather?

Ensuring security of work area

- Do you have all the keys/access cards you might require to secure or unlock your patrol route?
- Is your control room/staff room secure?

Communication with colleagues

- Have you done a radio check to ensure your communication equipment is working?
- Have you done a battery check to ensure your comms don't fail mid-patrol?
- Have you checked in with your colleagues for unusual activity on your route?
- If you are a lone worker, have you notified your supervisor you are about to patrol?

It is important to do a radio check to make sure your communication equipment is working.

2.3 Patrolling procedures and techniques

There are no right or wrong patrolling procedures. How you patrol will depend on what your client wants, the size of your team, your assignment instructions and the type of environment. Table 2SO.3 on page 85 outlines the things that you can do to ensure your patrol is effective.

Table 2SO.3: Effective patrol techniques

Technique	Description
Plan effectively	Your patrol route should be planned to include details of route variations, your timings, how often you patrol, and how long your route takes. This will enable you to retrace your steps at any point and pinpoint where on your route you were at any given time. Tour patrol systems monitor this information electronically.
Be systematic	Being systematic means being methodical on your patrol and associated duties. Ensure you check all areas of your route in sequence so you can be confident you haven't missed anything.
Use your senses	It can be difficult to remain alert after numerous patrols and it can be easy to miss vital details. Try to remain as alert as possible and use all your senses such as sight, smell and hearing while on patrol as you never know when an incident could occur.
Procedures for patrols of internal and external areas	Be aware that different procedures and requirements may exist in internal and external areas as the risks and security weaknesses may be very different.

Case study: Remaining alert

Jack is a new security officer with an established SIA registered security company in Newcastle.

"I'm quite new to the security industry. I've only been a security officer for the past three months to help pay my university tuition fees. I'd never worked nights before and I'd never been a lone worker before so it was a real shock to the system. The main problem for me was I was placed on a building site as the night duty officer and without anyone else to talk to or anything else to stimulate me I'd start to get drowsy and miss my designated patrol times. Even worse than that, when I did make it out on patrol I'd walk round and sometimes be off in a world of my own so that when I got back to the cabin I couldn't recall being at some of my check points even though I knew I must have walked past them. I knew I'd lose my job if I couldn't shape up so I set up a series of alerts on my phone so I would never miss a patrol and drew up a checklist so I physically had to tick off my checkpoints as I went round. Being organised like this really helped."

Over to you

1. Why was Jack struggling to do his job?

2. What else could Jack have done to help stay alert?

3. What could the security company have done to support Jack?

4. What are the consequences if Jack fails in his duties, both for him personally and for his company?

2.4 Equipment required for patrolling

The equipment you need for effective patrolling is shown in Figure 2SO.1 below and is also discussed in section 1.3 (page 80).

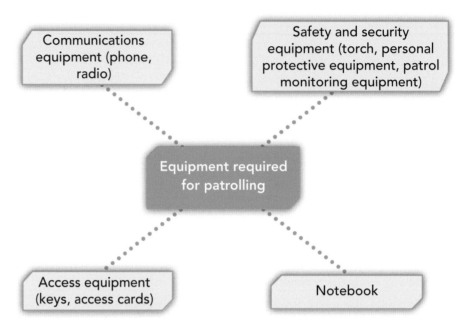

Figure 2SO.1: Equipment required for patrolling

Activity: Local site knowledge

You have been allocated to a three-month contract as part of a building site security team. The reason you and your colleague have been brought in is that the site has been suffering from continuous vandalism and materials theft which has cost the building company thousands of pounds and threatens their completion deadline. In order to ensure you and your team prevent any further disruptions and delays, what local and site knowledge would you need in order to plan your patrols?

2.5 Importance of vigilance and using local and site knowledge when patrolling

If you keep alert and research your site you will be a more effective security officer:

- **Better patrol planning** – by using local knowledge and keeping alert you will be able to plan your patrol route more effectively to deter and detect criminal or unauthorised activities.

- **Increased hazard awareness** – you will know what potential hazards face you on site and will be prepared to deal with them effectively, and in the process help keep yourself, your colleagues, the premises and the public safe.

- **Ability to deal with incidents and emergencies** – using site and local knowledge you will know which incidents are likely to occur and what your response should be.

3. Understand how to control access and egress from a site

As explained in section 1.1, control of access and egress is part of monitoring and allowing or restricting entry and exit from a business premises or site.

3.1 Purposes of access and egress control

There are three main reasons to control access and egress:

- **Maintaining safety of people on site** – Allowing too many people into premises such as an entertainment venue can cause a breach of fire regulations and, if there is an incident, could lead to people being trampled and seriously hurt. It is therefore important that the number of people inside a venue is controlled carefully. In addition, some premises contain high-value items or information, which would be a prime target for thieves. By controlling who has access to the site you can reduce the risk of theft.

- **Monitoring and control of movement of people and property** – By controlling and monitoring people and property you make it much easier to respond to emergency situations. In an evacuation scenario you would be able to advise the emergency services how many people were in a particular location and what hazardous equipment might be at risk from explosion or leakage. You also reduce the risk of theft or damage by monitoring.

- **Maintaining security of site and property** – One of your main roles when working as a security officer is to ensure your site is safe and property is not lost or stolen. Monitoring who comes in and out of premises is one possible method of reducing the risk that a site is damaged or property stolen.

3.2 Duties during access and egress control

If you are part of the security team responsible for access/egress control, or you are a lone worker with full responsibility for this aspect of security work, there are some key procedures you should know. However it is important to be aware that different companies and premises will have different procedures for controlling access and egress, so the information below is general guidance only.

Procedures for visitors and vehicles on entry/exit

You will have set procedures to follow if you are responsible for monitoring access and egress to premises. These procedures may involve any or all of the following:

- issuing visitor identification passes
- completing visitor registration forms
- recording vehicle licence numbers
- issuing vehicle passes
- performing identity checks on individuals
- performing searches of individuals and vehicles
- ensuring visitors follow instructions at the site.

Key control procedures

It is likely that you will have to follow specific procedures for the use and storage of keys. Remember that in this context a key can also be an access card or ID fob which allows access to certain areas. Duties relating to key control include:

- using and maintaining the security of a key safe
- checking keys in and out of a safe
- logging key bunches
- keeping a register of key issues and returns
- random and routine key checks.

Process by which access is denied

There will also be occasions where you will have to deny individuals entry to premises. In doing so you must follow the procedures detailed in your assignment instructions, which will be different for each employer. However you should remember at all times to remain professional and courteous and seek additional assistance if necessary.

3.3 Powers and identification requirements of statutory agencies

Although you must follow your assignment instructions in refusing entry to individuals, you must also be aware that there are agencies and organisations that have a right to enter the premises to conduct inspections and searches, either by a power issued to them in law or through a warrant. These organisations include:

- Police – may be looking for evidence of criminal activity, or individuals who are wanted for questioning

As part of a security team you may be responsible for using and maintaining the security of a key safe.

- HM Revenue and Customs – may be looking for illegal immigrants in the workforce, or evidence of tax fraud

- Health and Safety Inspectors – may be investigating serious breaches of health and safety law

- Environmental Health Inspectors – checking for compliance on health and hygiene issues

- Fire Officers – checking fire exits, maximum capacities, evacuation procedures and issuing safety certificates.

Signing-in and identification procedures

Although some organisations may have a right in law to enter the premises to carry out a search or assessment, this does not mean you simply allow them access. You must ensure that they are who they say they are by checking their identification thoroughly and ensuring they follow correct sign-in procedures, which may include photographs and searches. If in doubt, seek advice from your supervisor.

4. Understand basic search procedures

There will be occasions during your career where you will be required to search individuals or vehicles. Unlike the police you have no search powers so how this is conducted is of the utmost importance if you are to stay on the right side of the law.

4.1 Conditions to be in place before searching

Before any search takes place you must be sure of several things:

1. Is it part of employee contract/visitor terms of entry? – Is it clear to the public and visitors that they will be subject to a search procedure if they want to enter the premises? Is it actually a requirement of their entry to the premises? You can't just conduct a search because you choose to. It has to be a condition of entry set by your employer or client.

2. Is the search procedure part of your assignment instructions? – (Assignment instructions are discussed in section 1.2). Have you been tasked with searching people or vehicles on your daily instructions? Is it what your employer or client agreed as part of your duties?

3. You must secure consent from the person to be searched – You are not a police officer and you have no more powers than any other citizen. You cannot search someone who does not want to be searched. You can only search individuals or vehicles with consent from the person concerned. If they do not consent you do not have to allow them entry to the premises, but you cannot force them to submit to a search.

4.2 Different types of search

Your duties may require you to conduct different types of search for a variety of different reasons. The most common types of search you will encounter are described in Table 2SO.4 below.

Table 2SO.4: Common types of search

Search type	Description
Routine	A routine search is a standard approach set out by your assignment instructions. You would do this as a standard part of your job duties on a daily basis.
Intelligence-based	Intelligence-based searches are conducted on the basis of information you have received or observed about a specific issue. For example, if you received a call from a member of the public letting you know who was responsible for a series of workplace equipment thefts, you might approach that person specifically on the basis on this intelligence and search their office or vehicle.
People	Many organisations require visitors to undergo a person search before they can have entry. This might be a search for weapons, concealed recording equipment or any other prohibited or stolen items. Store detectives can ask to search a person if they suspect shoplifting.
Bags	A bag search is similar to a person search and may happen at the same time. The contents of a bag are either scanned or searched (or both) to ensure that the person isn't carrying prohibited or stolen items.
Vehicles	A vehicle search is a check of the vehicle a person arrives in. It may be conducted instead of or as well as a person and bag search. You will be looking for prohibited or stolen articles, or on some premises, you may even be looking for the threat of explosives.

4.3 Procedures for personal and vehicle searches

Searching a person or their property is an invasion of their privacy and they may feel uncomfortable about it even if they understand why it has to be done and they have agreed to it. There are things you can do as a security officer to make the process run smoothly and ensure the search is as straightforward as possible for yourself and for the person involved.

Professionalism in searches – be professional at all times when you are searching; remember you are representing your employer or their client. Consider the following during any search you do:

- Always ask the individual's permission before starting any search.

- Show empathy; it is uncomfortable for people to have their privacy invaded.

- Be polite and courteous at all times; treat the public as you would want to be treated yourself.

- Keep control of the process; don't allow others to observe what you are doing or interfere.

Did you know?

SCONE is an acronym that provides guidance on loss prevention to retail security officers.
- **S**eeing a person
- **C**oncealing an item
- **O**bserving them continuously
- **N**ot paying for the item
- **E**xiting the store

- Assist where necessary; some people may have mobility problems or large bags, so help them out if you can.

Best practice for searches – there will be a set of best practice measures for your searches which indicate how well you are doing; these may be industry standards or they may be set by your employer. When you try to meet or exceed those best practice measures consider the following:

- You can allow individuals to self-search. This involves asking them to open their bags or empty their pockets. It is less invasive than you doing it.

- Where you are conducting a person search you need to consider same-sex searching. Do you have the personnel to have female security officers search female visitors and male officers search male visitors? Some visitors or members of the public may be embarrassed if they are searched by a member of the opposite sex.

- Consider having a second member of staff present as a witness so that if a member of the public accuses you of inappropriate activity you have a source of third-party support.

- Do you have appropriate facilities to conduct a person search? Are you outside in inclement weather? Do you have indoor space to do this? If you require religious dress to be removed to facilitate a search, do you have a private space to do this in?

Procedures for vehicle searches – if you are responsible for a lot of vehicle searches you have to be efficient so that you don't hold up traffic to the business or premises, but thorough enough that you don't accidentally miss something important. You should consider the following:

- You can ask the individual to self-search their vehicle by asking them to open their boot, move cushions or seat covers or open the glove box.

- You should use a designated area for the search so that the vehicle is not blocking the passage of other traffic.

- You need to give clear instructions and information to the driver so they know exactly what to do and where to go.

- You should consider carefully which areas of a vehicle to search. The search areas will largely depend on what you are looking for. For example, if you were looking for a person hiding, the glove box would not be a realistic search area. Generally you might look in the boot, on the floor and seats and under the vehicle itself.

CCTV may be used on site to confirm the presence of a hazard or intruder.

4.4 Actions in the event of a refusal to be searched

Remember that you have no authority to search a member of the public or their property if they refuse to be searched. You can provide them with information about why the search needs to take place and its importance, but they can choose to say no. If you are faced with a refusal, under no circumstances should you force the issue, but equally the person should not be allowed entry if that is what is stated in your assignment instructions. You can ask the person for their name and address and the person whom they would like to visit at the premises, but equally they do not have to provide you with this information.

If the member of the public is calm and polite throughout their refusal, you should notify the circumstances to site management and a more senior representative may come to assist you in the situation or offer radio guidance. If the member of the public turns aggressive or threatening, you always have the option to call the police.

Case study: Body scanners

The Rapiscan x-ray search machine has been deployed at Heathrow and Manchester airports since 2009. It is a full-body scanner that produces an image of a person seemingly without their clothes. In March 2010 two Muslim women were randomly selected to undergo the body scan as a security measure before being allowed on an international flight to Islamabad in Pakistan. They refused on religious grounds and were consequently refused permission to fly by security staff. Civil liberties campaigners are concerned that these 'naked' scans are a breach of personal privacy and could be misused. The security industry argues that they exist to protect the public and that the images are deleted immediately and security staff are trained to respect the privacy of others.

Over to you

1. What are the possible reasons the female passengers refused the scan?

2. Do you think the scans are an invasion of privacy?

3. Do you think there is potential for security staff to misuse the scans?

4. Were the security staff right to refuse permission to fly in this case?

4.5 Information to be recorded in search documentation

Some security companies require formal documentation to be completed during each search. This is usually a straightforward proforma which looks similar to the example shown below:

Name:	Time and date:
Search type:	
Items found:	
Signature:	

Figure 2SO.2: Example of formal search documentation

Completing this properly is your evidence that the search was conducted appropriately and the forms should be logged safely on a daily basis in case any allegations or questions arise.

4.6 Action when property is found during a search

During your search you may find any number of prohibited or unauthorised articles. How you proceed at that point will depend on the type of article found and your company policy on the matter. In general you would consider the following procedures:

- **Contacting management** – you would contact your supervisor who would then make the decision what to do next. This may involve contacting the police depending upon the article found.

- **Retention of items found** – if the article is illegal or dangerous you would retain it and hand it over to the police as evidence. If it is just a prohibited article on the site, you might confiscate it for the duration of the visit and then return it as the visitor leaves.

Activity: Incident report

Consider an incident you have witnessed which is still relatively fresh in your mind. It could be one you were directly involved in or one you observed from a distance. Once you have chosen an incident write a report which addresses the following. (This exercise will also reinforce the need to carry a logbook while you are at work.)

- **Who** was involved? Try to record names, descriptions of the suspects, and any vehicles.
- **What** happened? Detail the events exactly as you saw them.
- **When** did it happen? What was the time and date of the incident?
- **Where** did it happen? Where were you specifically, what was the address or site location?
- **Why** did it happen? How did the incident arise and what was the end result?

- **Responses when people refuse to stay** – As mentioned previously, you don't have any powers over and above those of an ordinary member of the public so if a visitor decides to leave there may not be a lot you can do about it. Remember to remain polite and respectful at all times and call the police if required. You do have the option to make a citizen's arrest for some crimes such as theft or burglary, but if this is done incorrectly you will find yourself in court. If in any doubt leave arrests to the police – it is what they are trained for.

- **Information to be included in an incident report** – The information you provide is very important as incident reports are legal documents which the police may attach to their investigations and which can be used as evidence in court.

5. Understand the purpose and function of different types of technology, security and monitoring systems in the security environment

Security is increasingly becoming more technological and it is inevitable you will come across security technology in the course of your daily duties. This part of the course looks at the types of technology you might come across most frequently.

5.1 Types and main purposes of security and monitoring technology

The main purposes of security technology are the same as the main purposes of security personnel themselves, to protect the public, prevent loss, waste and damage, deter crime, provide emergency response and monitor entry and exit. Technology can do this in different ways:

- **Safety systems** – technologies which have a primary role in protecting the safety of people and property, such as fire alarms, smoke detectors and gas detectors.

- **Security systems** – technologies that exist primarily to secure property, such as intruder alarms and electronic article surveillance.

- **Safety and security systems** – combined systems which manage the safety and security of people and property, such as CCTV and access control systems.

Smoke detectors have a primary role of protecting the safety of people and property.

5.2 Features of security, monitoring and emergency systems

In your work as a security officer you will come across a variety of security and monitoring systems (see Table 2SO.5) and it is beneficial for you to know where they are likely to be found, how they are operated and how they might be activated.

Table 2SO.5: Types of emergency system

System	Description
Heat alarm system	Heat alarms are found in rooms or premises where smoke or mist are part of the normal working atmosphere which means normal smoke detectors would not be effective. They activate as a result of a rapid rise in temperature which might indicate a fire. The alarm is then triggered either at the site of the rise in temperature (alarm noises, flashing lights etc) or at an alarm centre which can send for the emergency services.
Smoke alarm system	Smoke alarms are detectors that measure particles in the atmosphere and trigger an alert either at the scene or at an alarm centre. You find smoke alarms in most businesses and homes as a matter of routine. Some smoke alarm systems are linked to fire control mechanisms such as those discussed in Unit 1 section 4.4.
Gas alarm system	Gas alarm systems provide early warning of the leakage of flammable or toxic gases. You will find them in premises where gases are used or produced as a by-product of a manufacturing process. They trigger when they measure gas concentrations above prescribed levels and give warnings via audible and visible signals. Like smoke and heat alarms, they can also be linked to an alarm centre which can take appropriate action such as evacuation procedures and emergency service contact.
Break-circuit intruder alarms	Many intruder alarms are built on the basis of a simple electrical circuit built into entryways such as doors or windows. When the door or window is opened the circuit is broken and the alarm triggered.
Infra-red intruder alarms	Infra-red detectors are used to detect a change in the temperature of an environment which might indicate an intruder has entered the premises. Once the intruder has been detected the alarm is produced either audibly or visibly or at an alarm centre.
Card swipe access systems	Swipe cards have the identification of a person and their permitted access encoded on a magnetic strip. The card is swiped through a reader which interprets the magnetic strip and then allows or refuses entry depending upon the information stored there. You find swipe cards at access points in many businesses as an access/egress control measure as it doesn't require monitoring personnel and is therefore cheaper than manned access control.
Key pad access control systems	These systems consist of a numerical keypad that opens a door or barrier when the correct numerical sequence is entered. They can be found on internal and external entrances to buildings.
Proximity access control systems	Proximity readers use smart cards which look like credit cards, but emit a signal which can be picked up and read by a proximity reader which then automatically unlocks or opens a door. They normally have a range of about 10cm and are commonly found on external gates and car park barriers as well as internal doors.
Electronic article surveillance	Electronic article surveillance (EAS) is primarily found in the retail sector. It involves an electronic tag being fitted to retail goods which is removed by the clerk when the goods are paid for. There are barriers at the entrance to the store which activate an alarm if they detect a tag passing between them.

5.3 Alarm system operator controls and indicators

Alarm systems for large premises can be complex and the control panel will be able to highlight activity in different zones of the building. These alarms usually have some key functions for you to be familiar with.

- **Alarm, zone and fault indicators** – these are the controls which indicate where an alarm has been sounded, which zone it is in and if there is a fault with the system. Faults are highlighted both from a repair point of view but also because intruder interference might cause a fault.

- **Mute, rest and reset switches** – most alarm systems include these functions: mute silences the alarm, the rest function temporarily turns the alarm off in particular area or zone, and the reset button silences the alarm and resets it. The ability to mute or rest an alarm is important as if you know you have a possible intruder the alarm has performed its function and there is no need to let it continue ringing, particularly if the business has neighbours and it is evening or night-time.

- **Disable/inhibit function** – this function allows some zones to be disabled or inhibited while allowing others to be maintained. This could be used when you need to move through certain parts of the building without switching the entire alarm system off.

Activity: Differences between alarms

At your college, training provider or place of work look at the alarm controls for the fire alarm system and intruder alarm system. Identify and explain the differences you can see.

5.4 Actions to be taken in response to alarm activations

The primary reason alarms exist is to trigger a response in the people who hears them. This might be to encourage the person who triggered the alarm to leave, or to notify the person who hears it to investigate or evacuate.

Responses to alarm activations

If an alarm is triggered, security personnel have several options they can take. They can do a site visit; this is often requested by an alarm control centre if the security personnel are patrolling across multiple sites. Security personnel situated on site may use CCTV to confirm the presence of a hazard or intruder and respond accordingly. Alarm activations should never be ignored.

Risks and hazards when responding to alarms

Security personnel should always ensure they follow procedures when investigating alarms. They must be aware of the dangers posed by intruders, toxic gas, fire, smoke and panicked employees. Failure to appreciate the risks and act accordingly can cost thousands of pounds in damage and potentially cost lives.

5.5 Meaning of the term 'false alarm'

False alarms can happen with any form of alarm technology. In this context it is taken to mean activation of the alarm without incident. The common causes of false alarms are:

- the alarm has not been installed properly
- the alarm has not been serviced regularly
- the system or parts of the system have failed
- user error
- electrical interference from external sources such as lightning.

6. Understand the law and its relevance to the role of a security officer

Although you are not a police officer, security officers have often been referred to as the private policing sector. You may not have the powers of a police officer, but it is important that you know enough about relevant legislation to be able to do your job properly.

6.1 Relevant legislation

Serious Organised Crime and Police Act 2005

One of the laws which provides the police with powers is the Serious Organised Crime and Police Act (SOCPA, 2005). Some of the key changes it made are described below:

- The Act created a serious organised crime squad to deal with the most severe crimes in society, such as human trafficking, which are often conducted by underworld gangs.
- It introduced significant changes to the powers of arrest.
- It banned public protest within a kilometre of Parliament. This was hugely controversial as the right to protest is a basic human right.

Key terms

Legislation – law which has been created and enacted by a governing body, such as the government.

Human trafficking – the movement of people across borders, usually by force or deception, in order to exploit them for financial gain.

Powers of arrest

The police power of arrest used to be set out in Section 24 of the Police and Criminal Evidence Act (PACE) 1984, but section 110 of SOCPA (2005) created a new general power of arrest and created code G of PACE which sets out the conditions where a police officer might choose to arrest. In summary these conditions are:

- to find out a person's name
- to find out a person's address
- to prevent a person from committing an offence
- to protect another person
- to allow investigation into the conduct of a person
- to make sure a person does not abscond.

Indictable and non-indictable offences

The list below describes the most common types of offence you are likely to come across in the course of your duties as a security officer.

- **Trespass** – Trespass most commonly means to interfere with a person's land; this might mean entering the land without permission. Trespass is not a criminal matter and you cannot be prosecuted for it in a criminal court.

- **Aggravated trespass** – This is a crime under the Criminal Justice and Public Order Act 1994. A person can be prosecuted under this law if they enter a person's property with the intention of disrupting lawful activity being carried out.

- **Theft** – This is a crime under the Theft Act 1968 and involves the taking of another's property with the intention of keeping it. It is a 'triable either way' offence which means, depending on how serious the offence is, it could go to either the Magistrates court or the Crown Court.

- **Burglary** – This is a crime under the Theft Act 1968. A person is guilty of burglary if they trespass on premises with intent to steal.

- **Criminal damage** – This is a crime under the Criminal Damage Act 1971. A person is guilty of criminal damage if they destroy or damage property belonging to another without a lawful reason.

- **Types of assault** – Assault is defined as a crime by the Criminal Justice Act 1988. It is the intentional causing of another person to fear that he will be subjected to unlawful violence. Battery is a term used when the violence is actually applied.

Key terms

Indictable offence – a serious criminal offence, which must be tried in Crown Court.

Non-indictable offence – a less serious crime, which is tried in a Magistrates' court. Also called a summary offence.

6.2 Correct procedure when dealing with a trespasser

Dealing with the issue of trespass can be difficult as it is a civil matter, not a criminal offence, so you can't threaten the trespasser with a criminal prosecution. You should consider the following key steps.

- **Confirming that trespass has occurred** – Are you sure the person is a trespasser? Could they have permission to be where they are? It is important to check so that you do not offend legitimate visitors to the site and harm your employer's reputation.

- **Dealing with trespassers who agree to leave** – This is normally very straightforward. If you ask a trespasser to leave and they agree to do so you should escort them to the nearest exit point and ensure they are aware of the potential civil consequences of trespassing, such as being sued. You may be required to collect their personal details, but they do not have to give you any information at all.

- **Dealing with trespassers who refuse to leave** – If you have asked the trespasser to leave and they have refused, the police will support you if the trespasser has damaged the property or has used threatening or abusive language. Property owners and their agents have the right to remove someone from their property using reasonable force. Reasonable force is discussed in section 6.4.

- **Keeping records** – Your employer will have incident logs and you yourself are likely to have a logbook. Trespassing incidents should be recorded in these logs. Usually you will be required to complete the 'who, what, when, where and why' of the incident.

Trespass can mean entering land without permission.

6.3 Arrest procedures

It is essential that security officers are confident about their powers of arrest to ensure they are acting lawfully when they are dealing with suspects. If they are not sure of their precise powers they could be the ones ending up in court. Security officers do not have any additional arrest powers over and above those of an ordinary citizen.

SOCPA (2005) states that all arrests must be justified. For security staff this justification would come in two ways:

1. It was not reasonably practical for a police officer to make the arrest instead.

2. The arrest itself was necessary to prevent the arrestee from:
   - causing physical injury to themselves or another person
   - suffering injury through their actions
   - causing loss or damage to property
   - escaping before the police arrive.

In order to make a lawful arrest, a security officer must believe that both of the above reasons apply. Table 2SO.6 outlines the main differences between a citizen's arrest and a police arrest.

Table 2SO.6: Key differences between citizen's arrests and police arrests

Citizen's arrests	Police arrests
Under PACE S24A (discussed in section 6.1) you cannot make a citizen's arrest if you believe a crime is *about to be* committed, only if one is being committed or has been committed.	The police can arrest if they believe a crime is *about to be* committed.
Citizens, and therefore security officers, can only arrest another person for 'indictable' offences. These are more serious offences such as theft, assault, robbery, burglary and some criminal damage.	The police can arrest for any offence.
Citizen's arrests are not carried out often and should not be carried out at all if there is a risk of danger or violence. In such circumstances the safest thing to do is to call the police and allow them to do their job.	The majority of arrests are made by the police. The police are trained to carry out arrests where there is a risk of danger or violence.

If you do carry out a citizen's arrest, you will need to bear in mind the following:

- **Information to give to the person being arrested** – You must make certain the suspect knows who you are and what you have arrested them for and make sure the police are notified at the earliest possible opportunity.

- **How to deal with people who resist arrest** – As discussed in section 6.4 you may use reasonable force to make an arrest. It is important to remember that if your version of events and the version given by the suspect are different, you could find yourself in court charged with an offence (see the Omari Roberts case study on page 101 for more information). It you think a suspect may resist, consider your own safety first and call the police.

- **Facilities and monitoring required after arrest** – In order for a citizen's arrest to be lawful, the suspect must be taken to the police or magistrate's court within a reasonable time. This effectively means as soon as you possibly can. In the intervening time you should ensure the comfort and welfare of your arrestee.

6.4 Reasonable use of force

In England and Wales anyone can use reasonable force to protect themselves or others, carry out an arrest or prevent a crime from occurring. The basis of this law is in the Criminal Law Act 1967. The difficult part of using force against intruders or trespassers is in deciding what is 'reasonable'. Reasonable force is not what the individual themselves decides is reasonable; the definition of 'reasonable' is decided by a jury and is unique in every case. If you use force in the course of your duties you must be absolutely certain that you have used the minimum amount of force you needed to avert the situation.

Ask yourself the following questions before you use force:

1. Is it absolutely necessary? Can the situation be averted in any other way?

2. Is your response proportionate to the situation?

Case study: Omari Roberts

Omari Roberts was 23 years old when he was violently confronted by two armed teenage burglars while visiting his mother's home in 2009. Mr Roberts picked up a kitchen knife to defend himself and fatally wounded 17-year-old Tyler Juett and injured his 14-year-old accomplice. He was charged with murder by the Crown Prosecution Service (CPS) after the 14-year-old burglar denied being armed and claimed he was running away when he was attacked by the defendant. Mr Roberts called 999 at the scene and administered CPR at the direction of the emergency services and tried to save Mr Juett's life until the emergency services arrived and took over. The CPS dramatically dropped the case when the 14-year-old admitted he had been armed and had not been running away. He also confessed to a social worker that he would have killed Mr Roberts if he'd had the chance.

Over to you

1. Why did the CPS charge Mr Roberts with murder?

2. Why was the word of the 14-year-old burglar accepted over the word of Mr Roberts?

3. What is your view of Mr Roberts' use of force in this situation? Was it reasonable, necessary and proportionate?

4. What would you have done in similar circumstances?

6.5 Different types of evidence

You may come across different types of evidence in the course of your duties. The main types are described in Table 2SO.7 below.

Activity: Reasonable use of force

Consider the following situations and responses. Decide whether the use of force in each one was 'reasonable', 'necessary' and 'proportionate'.

1. A security officer is patrolling at night and finds a woman sleeping under tarpaulin on the site. When he tries to wake her she becomes scared and runs away; he gives chase and tackles her to the ground. She is dazed and suffers cuts and bruises.

2. A store detective challenges a suspected shoplifter outside a store. The shoplifter pulls out a knife and threatens to stab the detective. The detective kicks the knife out of the suspect's hand and restrains him until the police arrive.

3. A group of teenagers are making a nuisance of themselves in a shopping centre. A security officer challenges them and asks them to leave, but they respond by laughing and shouting. One of the young people takes the security officer's hat and starts throwing it around. The security guard grabs the youngster in a restraint hold and marches him to the exit.

Table 2SO.7: Types of evidence

Types of evidence	Description
Direct	Direct evidence is information that is objectively true and supports the guilt or innocence of a person. It could be evidence such as CCTV footage, audio tapes, DNA and some types of witness testimony.
Circumstantial	This is evidence that strongly suggests something, but isn't objectively true. It requires reasoning to draw probable conclusions.
Expert	This is evidence provided by someone who is deemed to be an expert in their field, such as a medical professor.
Hearsay	This is evidence that was heard second hand. It relates to what a witness was told by another rather than what they themselves heard or saw.
Documentary	This is evidence in the form of written or printed documents which support a person's innocence or guilt. It could consist of letters, notes or confessions.

6.6 Actions when preserving evidence

If a crime is committed on premises you are responsible for, you have a duty to preserve the evidence until the police and forensic specialists arrive. This includes:

Preventing contamination of crime scenes

You need to restrict access to the affected areas by using a cordon to block the area. You can set up a cordon easily with equipment you might normally have to hand such as cones, security tape or similar. This prevents the crime scene being contaminated and gives the police more chance to catch the culprit. You should stay at the scene until the police arrive to ensure that there is no unauthorised access by individuals who might want to interfere with the evidence. If your crime scene is outdoors you may also need to protect evidence from the weather: footprint and tyre prints can be destroyed by heavy rain, so consider covering them with plastic sheeting to preserve them until they can be recorded by the specialists.

Ensuring continuity of evidence

It is important if you are involved in collecting evidence that you keep an accurate record of what you have found, when you found it and the circumstances in case the evidence is required in court. It is also important that you use evidence bags, which should be clearly labelled and stored securely so that no tampering can take place.

Restrict access to the affected areas by using a cordon to block the area.

6.7 Reporting procedures following a crime

Knowing the procedures regarding reporting a crime is crucial if the culprit is to be caught and prevented from committing similar offences elsewhere.

- **When to report** – Report the crime as soon as you become aware that it has happened. If the crime is non-emergency then you can report it using the police 101 number. You should only dial 999 if there is a current danger to life and property.

- **Who to report to** – For non-emergency crime you should report to your supervisor who will speak with the customer and decide on a course of action which may include contacting the police. For emergency crime, where there is a current threat to life and property, you should ask your control room to contact 999 for an emergency police response.

- **What to report** – you should report the time, location and nature of the crime along with any other details that are asked of you by the police control room.

7. Understand the importance and purpose of reporting and record keeping

Accurate record keeping is essential in the execution of a security officer's job. The record can be used in court as evidence so it must be clear and professional.

7.1 Different types of records

Totally Safe Security Ltd

Assignment		Date	
On-duty security officers		Keys checked by	
Mobile radios		Torches	

I certify that I have read and understand the assignment instructions and have read the shift handover log.
Signature: _____

1. Doors or windows open / broken?	Y/N	4. Property damaged?	Y/N	7. Accidents?	Y/N
2. Electrical appliances on?	Y/N	5. Trespasser / suspicious activities?	Y/N	8. Visitors?	Y/N
3. Fire hazards?	Y/N	6. Thefts committed / attempted?	Y/N	9. Complaints	Y/N

Use the section below to report all occurrences that take place during your hours of duty.

Occurrence no.	Time	Description

Figure 2SO.3: A sample daily occurrence log

You will come across different types of records in your day-to-day duties; the ones that are your responsibility should be highlighted on your assignment instructions. The following are the common types of records you will have to keep:

- Incident reports – These log any significant incident such as first aid incidents, unauthorised entry or criminal activity.

- Search register – This is a record of the searches you have conducted and anything you found.

- Visitors register – This is a log of all visitors in and out of a site. Usually it will contain the vehicle registration number of each visitor's car, their name and the company they are representing.

- Key register – This is a log of keys in and out of a central location. It enables keys to be tracked and monitored for safety and insurance purposes.

- Notebook – You would normally keep your own notebook or log book to record any events, incidents or useful information as you patrol.

- Daily occurrence book – This is a log of your patrols, visits and incidents which happen during your assignment period.

- Accident book – This records any accidents or first aid incidents.

7.2 Dos and don'ts of report writing

The ability to write a clear and accurate report is a key skill every security officer should have. This means you should have strong literacy skills and it is likely that in order to be appointed to a security position you will need to prove you can write a good report. Figure 2SO.4 below includes some of the key considerations you should be aware of and Table 2SO.8 (on page 105) gives further information about them.

Figure 2SO.4: Some of the key elements to be aware of when writing a report

Table 2SO.8: Features of effective report writing

Feature of report	Description
Planning and structuring	Security officers' reports are normally completed on a proforma such as a daily occurrence log so your planning and structuring in terms of what to write and in what order is done for you. Ensure you complete all the boxes accurately and that you plan your time to allow for the report to be done when your shift finishes. Taking notes in your log book as you complete your rounds is essential for this – do not rely on your memory at the end of your assignment period.
Content and quantity of information	Keep your information simple and clear, avoid the use of shorthand or slang as your records will be read by others and could be used in court as well. Keep your information as factual as possible and use the 'who, what, when, where, why' principles. Do not add your own personal commentary as it looks unprofessional.
Timescales	Ensure your reports are completed in a timely fashion in accordance with your assignment instructions or in accordance with the specified guidance on the report form itself. Always sign and date your reports.
Recipients	Your supervisor or admin team are likely to take responsibility for gathering and storing reports, but remember they can be looked at by your clients at any time and can be used by the police as evidence in court.

7.3 Importance of an incident report

The completion of incident reports is discussed in 7.1. They are very important documents for several reasons, some of which are included in Table 2SO.9 below.

Table 2SO.9: Reasons why incident report documents are important

Reason	Explanation
Protection of the security guard	By logging and recording everything you do or see during your shift you protect yourself from allegations that you are not doing your job properly or from allegations of malpractice from the public.
Protection of the organisation	Security companies rely on their security officers' reports as proof that they are delivering the service they promised their client. A clear, accurate and timely report ensures their business reputation is protected and is also proof that you are protecting their client's business.
Possible use as evidence	Your incident reports may be the difference between conviction and acquittal for a criminal. It is vital that your reports are accurate and reliable to ensure the right people are punished.
Auditing and provision of monitoring information	Like any other business, security firms are monitored as part of quality review processes that highlight how well the firm is doing on the management of its service delivery. If reports aren't completed accurately and on time the company will be failing its customers and may lose contracts.

7.4 Information to record in an incident report

Information covered in incident reports is already mentioned in sections 4.6 and 7.2. A good report should include information about the incident, those involved, witnesses and actions taken as well as covering information about you and your role. The key pieces of information to be aware of are:

- Who
- What
- When
- Where
- Why.

Activity: Notebook use

Effective notebook use is a skill that can take some practice. Notebooks are available to buy in most stationery shops and online. If you are not yet working in the security industry one of the best ways to practise is to keep a notebook of your current day-to-day activity as it will get you into good habits which you can demonstrate to a security company at interview.

Security companies often have their own protocols for maintaining and completing notebooks

7.5 Dos and don'ts of notebook use

Specific security companies may have their own protocols for maintaining and completing notebooks. Some security companies may not require them at all for control room or reception-based staff. However it is very likely that they will be issued to all patrolling staff to act as a memory aid and as a record of their activities for a specified time period; they are also likely to be countersigned by a supervisor at the end of a shift.

How to make entries

Entries in a notebook would normally start with a clear record of the day and date and end with a solid line and a signature so that anyone reviewing the book is clear where each separate entry begins and ends. Entries would revolve around the 'who, what, when, where, why' principles and may include diagrams or location plans if required. The notebook should be completed 'in situ' to record the security officer's account of events at the time of the incident. It should not be completed after the events or at the end of your shift before you clock off.

Dealing with corrections

Information should not be removed from a notebook as it may give the impression of trying to hide information or evidence. If you make an incorrect entry or factual error then cross it out clearly with a single line so the text can still be seen and insert the new information and initial it to prove you are the one who added it. This helps prevent fraudulent entries.

How to deal with pages left blank in error

Blank spaces in notebooks are not permitted as they have the potential to lead to fraudulent entries. If a page is left blank in error it should be marked as 'left blank in error' with a strikethrough line across the page to prevent any additional entries being placed in the space.

Information that should not be recorded

Notebooks are not a minute-by-minute account of a security officer's shift. If nothing of note happens then it is acceptable just to record the time and date of patrol visits. Notebooks should also not be used to record personal observations or non-factual comments. It is an auditable book and can be used in court so keep it as accurate and professional as you can.

7.6 Content and importance of a handover

The handover at the end of your shift is a very important part of your job as it provides an opportunity for you to provide your relief with all the information and equipment they need in order to ensure continuity of security for your customer. This continuity is crucial: if you do not discuss the incidents you have encountered that day with the next shift they may be at risk of injury or not being able to protect the public or premises to best effect. You would normally hand over items such as essential documents and information, keys, logs, passwords if required and any equipment that is shared rather than yours alone.

7.7 Phonetic alphabet

The phonetic alphabet is used to ensure the intelligibility of voice signals over radio. The letters are used to spell out words so there can be no mistaking letter sounds such as 'm' and 'n'. The words linked to each letter are as shown in Table 2SO.10:

Table 2SO.10: The NATO phonetic alphabet

A = Alpha	N = November
B = Bravo	O = Oscar
C = Charlie	P = Papa
D = Delta	Q = Quebec
E = Echo	R = Romeo
F = Foxtrot	S = Sierra
G = Golf	T = Tango
H = Hotel	U = Uniform
I = India	V = Victor
J = Juliet	W = Whiskey
K = Kilo	X = X-ray
L = Lima	Y = Yankee
M = Mike	Z = Zulu

Just checking

1. Identify three responsibilities of a security officer.

2. What are assignment instructions?

3. Name two items you might be required to take on patrol.

4. Identify three types of security patrol.

5. Define access and egress.

6. When can you search a member of the public?

7. What should you do if a member of the public refuses a search?

8. Briefly describe two electronic safety systems.

9. What is the definition of a false alarm?

10. What do SOCPA and PACE stand for, and what are they?

11. What are the differences between a police arrest and a citizen's arrest?

12. Briefly describe four different types of evidence.

13. What are the five 'Ws' of report writing?

14. How should you deal with corrections in a notebook?

15. How would you spell 'security' over a radio using the NATO phonetic alphabet?

Dan Fielding
Security officer at a large university

Shift handovers can be really rushed. You have one team clocking out and one team clocking on and you have to be really organised if you are going to make sure you pass all the information over to your replacement. On this particular occasion my relief turned up late – according to our assignment instructions, we have to be on site and prepared to handover 10 minutes before the start of a shift. I was a bit angry to be honest as it meant I would be late getting away and I'd booked a table for my wife's birthday.

When he finally came in I gave him a few choice words, the keys and the visitor book and left as quickly as I could. I was halfway home when I realised I hadn't told him about an incident with a peeping tom earlier in the shift. We have large halls of residence on campus and there had been reports of a bloke trying to peek in some of the ground floor flats with female residents. I pulled over and called him on his mobile to let him know. My colleague went out to the halls and was able to apprehend the bloke trying to break into one of the flats. If I hadn't called him then this bloke would have been waiting for one of the girls in the flats and I dread to think what would have happened. It was a wake-up call for both me and my colleague that night – you don't skimp on your handovers; if you do someone might get hurt.

Over to you

1. What kind of information would you need to pass over in an effective handover?
2. What are the potential consequences of a poor handover?
3. What could have happened if Dan hadn't called his colleague?
4. Why do you think assignment instructions request you arrive before your allotted shift?

3 Conflict management for the private security industry

This unit is intended for security personnel such as door supervisors and security officers who need an SIA licence in order to be employed. The unit will cover avoiding and managing conflict in typical security situations such as commercial premises, industrial premises and entertainment venues.

The key focus of the unit is avoiding conflict in the first place, so understanding techniques to defuse conflict is very important. However you won't always be able to prevent or defuse conflict so you will also need to learn how to manage conflict and solve problems as they arise. This unit will also examine what should happen after conflict has been dealt with and how to share good practice.

Learning outcomes

After completing this unit you should:

1. understand the principles, communication skills and knowledge of conflict management appropriate to your role
2. understand how to recognise, assess and reduce risk in conflict situations
3. understand how to communicate effectively in emotive situations and de-escalate conflict
4. understand how to develop and use problem-solving strategies for resolving conflict
5. understand good practice to follow after conflict situations.

Security alert!

Conflict management

Most people encounter conflict fairly regularly in their own lives. This can range from disagreements with colleagues, conflict with a spouse, partner or parent, or refereeing arguments between children. Conflict itself is neither good nor bad; it is a natural and normal part of life. The key thing that determines whether conflict ends up being a positive or negative experience is how we deal with it.

Consider the last time you were in a conflict situation and make notes on how you approached it, what you did, what you said, your body language and attitude. How do you think your approach helped or hindered the situation?

1. Understand the communication skills and knowledge of conflict management appropriate to your role

Effective communication skills are a key quality required in any security personnel. They help you communicate with managers, colleagues, clients, customers and members of the public. This enables you to be more effective in your job.

1.1 Importance of positive communication to avoid conflict

Key term

Conflict – a struggle between people or groups with opposing ideas, needs, wants or beliefs.

Conflict can be triggered by differences of opinion, differences in values, differences in interpreting a situation and differences in understanding: when people don't agree, conflict can arise. Clear and effective communication can help defuse conflict before it becomes a problem. It is far better to prevent the escalation of conflict than to deal with the aftermath of it.

The importance of constructive communication

Often the root of conflict is a simple misunderstanding, so it is really important that your communication with colleagues, managers and the public is clear and constructive. You should never play with words by using irony or sarcasm while on duty as they can easily be misinterpreted and can provoke further conflict. You should always try to be as clear, calm and specific as possible and check that the person you are dealing with has understood what you are saying to them. Clear and constructive information sets out expectations of behaviour. You cannot just assume that everyone you deal with in your role will know how to behave appropriately; sometimes you must tell them.

How to communicate

You should communicate in a way that is clear, professional, polite and fair. If you are angry or emotional then this will come across to your audience and possibly provoke greater conflict. Remember that you are a professional security operative; your interactions with the public are not personal so it is not appropriate to treat them in the way you might deal with a friend or family member. You should be courteous and respectful at all times.

You should communicate in a way that is courteous and respectful at all times.

1.2 Importance of employer policies, guidance and procedures

Most good employers will have policies, procedures and guidance in place to help you deal with conflict that arises in the execution of your duties. The policies are usually drawn up based on legal advice and best practice in the sector, as companies know that if they provide incorrect guidance to their staff they can be legally liable if anything goes wrong. These policies are important as they can help you in the following ways:

1. If you follow the company policy to the letter then you have done exactly what your employer requires of you, leading to a reduced risk of being sued by a member of the public.

2. Following the policy also reduces the risk of harm to yourself and others.

3. The policy should clearly state what your role and responsibilities are in preventing and resolving conflict so you are aware of what you are required to do.

4. The policies may also provide you with a variety of options to take in particular circumstances so they act as a valuable tool in deciding the best course of action in a conflict situation.

1.3 Factors that can trigger an angry response

Anger is an emotional response to an unpleasant or threatening situation. It can be a way of overcoming perceived or actual injustice or powerlessness. Anger has some common triggers that you need to keep in mind – to be effective, you will have to prevent your own anger making a conflict situation worse, and help to reduce anger in others. Table 3.1 (on page 112) outlines some common triggers.

Table 3.1: Common triggers that can worsen conflict situations.

Common triggers	Description
Feeling threatened	If you feel threatened by a situation or an individual, a common reaction is to get angry about it. Anger often makes people feel more powerful and in control. For this reason, it's important that security personnel don't make people feel threatened. Remember that you may be seen as threatening without realising it: factors such as a uniform, radio, your size, your tone of voice, the number of colleagues surrounding you and your facial expression can combine to create threat even where none was intended.
Loss of face	Loss of face is a feeling of humiliation or loss of status in the eyes of others and it can lead to an angry response. It is important that you do not belittle people in the course of your job if you are to prevent conflict. Be polite and respectful at all times.
Frustration	One of the most common triggers for anger is frustration. People can get frustrated very easily when they don't feel they are being taken seriously or they don't have the information they require. When you are dealing with the public always try to minimise frustration by being clear about things like waiting times and provide as much information as you can about a situation so people can prepare themselves.
Physical discomfort	People will get angry if they suffer physical discomfort or they watch the discomfort of their friends and family. This might include things such as long queues in poor weather to get into a venue, a crush at the bar or pushing and shoving. Even something as simple as treading on someone's foot in a crowded venue can lead to angry conflict.

Factors that can increase likelihood of triggering an angry response

There are some factors that you can't control, such as alcohol or drugs, which can lead to an increased chance of conflict arising. However, just because you can't control them doesn't mean you can't deal with the situation more effectively as long as you know these factors are present.

Alcohol has a variety of different effects on people. If you are working in the security industry as a door supervisor or retail security guard you are likely to come into contact with the after-effects of alcohol consumption on a regular basis. Alcohol can cause high levels of aggression in some people and an increased risk of violence.

Alcohol can affect the way we process social information, leading us to misunderstand situations and misread social cues. Alcohol also has the added side effect of making people more relaxed and less anxious, but this can lead to trouble as anxiety is our natural early warning of a threatening situation. If our anxiety is reduced we may not see a threat when it appears. The design of some pubs, clubs and bars can also lead to heightened aggression and violence.

Did you know?

Each week in the UK there are approximately 23,000 alcohol-related violence incidents and more than a third of these incidents happen in or around pubs and clubs.

"Busy pubs and bars can often experience friction points where customers brush up against one another and invade each other's personal space. This can quickly lead to frustration and escalate to aggression, especially where customers have been drinking or where there is an expectation of aggression. Some venue environments are more 'charged' than others and staff must always be on the look-out for such risks."

ASNED (the Association of Sustainable Night-time Economy Development)

The effects of **drugs** can be unpredictable, particularly if the drugs are mixed with alcohol. Some drugs can lead to anger, paranoia and hallucinations, leading to increased levels of conflict which you will have to deal with. The drugs you are likely to come into contact with as a security officer or door supervisor are:

- **Ecstasy** – This drug can have unpredictable effects and in a club environment can lead to a person overheating and becoming dehydrated. Collapses from ecstasy are not uncommon and can cause fear and panic among the peer group of the person who has collapsed. This will mean you have to deal with a casualty in a first aid situation and also with a group of disorientated and frightened friends – this can trigger conflict.

- **Cannabis** – This drug can cause sensory distortions and mild hallucinations in high doses, which in places like bars or clubs can lead to unusual or inappropriate behaviour. When mixed with alcohol it can also cause vomiting, which may cause conflict with others.

- **Cocaine** – This is a stimulant and can lead to overconfidence; people who take it may make poor decisions about how to deal with situations. If you feel invincible you may engage in conflict thinking you cannot be beaten and security staff and door supervisors often have to pick up the pieces after such poor decisions, in terms of both first aid and conflict resolution.

Activity: Drugs and conflict

Consider the following drugs you may come across if you work in the security industry in a club, pub or bar setting:
- Amphetamines
- Magic mushrooms
- Ketamine
- LSD

Research the effects of these drugs on the body and behaviour of individuals and answer the following questions:

1. How might they increase the likelihood of conflict?

2. What impact could each drug have on how you deal with someone who has taken it?

Personality – Some people are more prone to engaging in disagreement than others because they are more prone to losing their temper or reacting badly to opposition. If your temper is an issue you may want to consider what you can do to develop control over it. A hot-tempered security operative is a liability for a reputable security company because a poor response to conflict from you could lead to the loss of their reputation, valuable contracts and possibly even find them in court.

Did you know?

About 40% of people who are admitted to accident and emergency departments have alcohol-related injuries or illnesses.

Did you know?

There have been over 200 ecstasy-related deaths in the UK since 1996.

Did you know?

A good source of information about the types of drugs commonly used by clubbers and their effects can be found at the Talk to Frank website. For a link, please visit www.pearsonhotlinks.co.uk.

Medical conditions

There are some medical conditions that can affect a person's behaviour and how they might approach or deal with conflict situations. You will not know whether the people in a conflict situation are mentally or physically ill, but following sound conflict management techniques such as effective and constructive communication and your company's policies and guidance will help you with difficult situations.

1.4 Factors that can inhibit an angry response

As you are likely to have to deal with situations and environments that trigger angry responses, you need to be familiar with the factors that can help calm situations down. These can be useful tools when dealing with conflict in your workplace, as described in Table 3.2 below.

Table 3.2: Factors that can inhibit angry responses

Factor	Explanation
Self-control	Anger and violence can escalate, so if you remain controlled and professional you are likely to get a more controlled response from others – or at the very least prevent an already angry situation from escalating.
Fear of confrontation	Confrontation can be difficult and it takes confidence and practice in order to handle it well. Many people are genuinely afraid of confrontation and this can be a useful tool when you are dealing with people in a conflict situation.
Retaliation or other consequences	Some people will avoid conflict situations because they are afraid of the possible consequences such as being prosecuted, being banned from premises or being reported to an employer.
Peer pressure	Peer pressure can be a very effective way of inhibiting conflict; even if one person is angry and upset it may be that the presence of their family, friends or partner keeps them from getting out of hand. Alternatively the family, friends or partner may directly calm the situation down by removing the angry person from the vicinity of the problem.
Previous experience	People are often wiser with experience. If creating a scene or conflict hasn't worked successfully in the past they will know there is no point doing it now. This is why in the security industry it is particularly important for you and your teams to be consistent in your response to conflict.

Case study: Conflict patterns

Ali is a door supervisor at an exclusive combined restaurant and club in Manchester.

"It's normally reasonably quiet during the week; you get very little trouble as the clientele are normally a little bit older and we have some corporate functions. On Friday and Saturday it becomes much more of a challenge and we have much larger teams working those nights. One Friday we had a large group of premier league footballers in with their girlfriends and mates. Footballers are normally really well behaved because their club would fine them if there was trouble and there are always press outside waiting to take pictures of any incidents for the Sunday papers. The trouble normally comes from the drunken lads who see these footballers with the money, the champagne and the girls and think they'd like to be the one to take them down a peg or two. On this particular night a group of lads had insulted a footballer's girlfriend on her way back from a trip to the ladies' toilets and it escalated really quickly into a drunken brawl. A couple of colleagues and I got to the scene pretty fast as we had been notified on our earpieces by the in-club CCTV operator. When we intervened in the conflict the footballers backed off immediately, but the group of drunken lads were completely up for a fight. We couldn't defuse the situation, so in the end we escorted them off the premises and called the police."

Over to you

1. What are the benefits of Ali knowing the conflict pattern at his club on particular days of the week and with particular clientele?

2. In this particular situation, why were the footballers a possible target for conflict?

3. When Ali and his colleagues intervened what were the factors that made the footballers back off?

4. What factors might have increased the possibility of an angry response in this situation?

1.5 Managing customer expectations to reduce the risk of conflict

Customers have a right to expect a certain standard of service when they visit commercial or business premises and if those standards are not met it can provoke an angry response and potentially lead to conflict. The key to reducing the conflict is to ensure customers are realistic about what to expect.

A long wait to get into a club can make people feel frustrated and angry.

Unrealistic expectations about a situation

If customers or members of the public do not understand the reality of a situation and have a false impression of what will happen then conflict can ensue.

> "The club had booked a band to play and the weather was shocking: there was a gale blowing and the rain was sheeting down. The queue to get in the club was about 200 strong and people were starting to get upset at being out in the cold. I don't blame them, but just because it's raining doesn't mean we change how we admit people to the club and the searches we do. They should have had some sense and brought a coat and umbrella, in my opinion."
>
> *Jarvis Markham – Door supervisor*

The quote from a door supervisor above indicates that the crowd had unrealistic expectations and this led to anger and conflict, which ultimately the club security staff had to deal with.

Managing expectations

Providing information can help manage customer expectations. If the public know what to expect in a given situation they will be more likely to adjust to it and there will be less conflict. The kind of information you should consider providing includes things such as:

- **How long they may be required to wait** – This is a key piece of information for any member of the public who has to queue to gain access to a facility or premises. People are more likely to be patient if they know how long they have to wait; they can then make an informed choice whether to continue queuing or move on to another venue. In addition you will deal with less conflict on the door. It can be a good idea to assign a member of staff to walk up and down the queue to ensure everyone is aware of the situation.

- **Company policy** – Sometimes the public won't realise that things have to be done in a certain way because it is dictated by company policy. If you explain you are following policy, they may be less inclined to think your actions are personal and be calmer about the situation. It is also really important to do this at the earliest opportunity. If you have 500 people queuing for a club it is better to tell them they don't meet the dress code when they join the queue rather than when they have been waiting for an hour.

- **Your own expectations** – It is important to be clear about what you expect from people and what people can expect from you. If you tell someone you expect a search to take two minutes and you expect them to be cooperative and polite, they are more likely to be so.

Activity: Unrealistic expectations

Can you think of a situation where you have been angry or involved in conflict because something didn't live up to your expectations? If you are currently employed in the security industry, can you think of a situation where you have had to deal with unrealistic members of the public? What can you do to reduce or defuse the situation?

1.6 Human responses to emotional and threatening situations

The human body has adapted to dealing with emotional and threatening situations. These responses are primitive and developed through thousands of years of evolution. The responses you see or exhibit in conflict situations are essentially the same mechanisms that warned our ancestors about predators and created a response that kept them safe.

Common responses

Some of the most common responses to stressful or threatening situations are fear, anger and aggression. These responses can appear singly or a person can exhibit all three at the same time. Being put in a frightening situation can make people very angry especially if they are concerned for their own safety or the safety of a companion; this can lead them to become very aggressive and they seek to overcome the original threat by causing threat in return. This very quickly leads conflict situations to escalate out of control.

The fight, flight or freeze response

The primitive responses to situations of acute stress taken by your sympathetic nervous system are fight, flight or freeze. These responses are hardwired into your brain as a survival mechanism and can affect someone's behaviour in ways that they did not predict and do not feel they have control over.

Fight – When we are under acute stress we release hormones into our body, such as **adrenaline**, that make us stronger. These hormones, combined with the fear of the situation, may lead us to fight the source of the stress, whether this is a situation or a person. These hormones can lead even the most mild-mannered person into an all-out ferocious battle with more strength and aggression than they ever thought possible. As a security operative you must control this response so that you don't injure members of the public when you feel threatened and only ever use a reasonable level of force in controlling a situation.

Flight – This is escaping from the source of stress by moving or running away from a situation. The chemicals triggered by stress can make humans faster and more resilient to pain meaning that we can escape even if we are injured or wounded. This is a very common response to a threatening event but, unlike ordinary members of the public, you may not have the option to flee from dangerous situations: you are paid and employed to resolve them and call for emergency service assistance if you cannot. There will be occasions when the safety of the public is dependent on you overcoming this reflex.

Key term

Adrenaline – a hormone produced by the adrenal glands which is naturally produced in stressful situations.

Activity: Controlling your responses

There will be times when you have to overcome your nervous system's responses to stressful situations in order to do your job and protect the public. There are some techniques you can use to help you stay on top of your responses:

1. Keep up-to-date on the most recent security literature on physical intervention and conflict management.

2. Attend regular training events; if your employer won't pay for them, consider paying for them yourself. Your safety could depend on it.

3. Develop confidence and skill: watch how experienced security officers deal with situations, ask them for advice or a critique of situations you have dealt with.

4. Understand fight, flight, and freeze so that you know what response your body is likely to take. You can then work on controlling that response.

5. Practise as often as you can, you can do this as role-plays with colleagues or just as part of a 'What if' written journal.

117

Freeze – This might seem counter-intuitive, but freezing can be a very successful survival mechanism in mammals. If you freeze the aggressor you are dealing with might move on elsewhere or give up on an assault altogether. One of the interesting things about the freeze reflex is that it can happen without warning even to experienced security personnel.

Case study: The freeze response

Jackson is the head of security for a live music venue.

"I was sitting in the staff room having a five-minute break and a coffee when a radio call came in from a member of my team that a couple who had been refused entry to the venue earlier in the evening had returned and the bloke was waving a nail-studded cricket bat around and threatening the door staff and the public. I put my coffee down and reached for the radio to tell them I was on my way and start to coordinate the response. Something happened to me that never happened before and has never happened since – my hand just froze on the radio, I couldn't move at all.

I couldn't believe it. I'm 6 feet 5 inches tall and I've been working in security for 15 years and I've dealt with situations which have been life threatening but I just couldn't move. My heart was racing like I'd run a marathon, my eyes were watering and I kept thinking what would I say if someone came in and saw me sitting there. I was just in a state of pure terror. About five minutes later the call came through that the bloke had been restrained and the police were on their way. I was shocked and embarrassed by my response, and my team still don't know the real reason I didn't respond – I've never spoken about it to anyone."

Over to you

1. Why did Jackson freeze?

2. How could Jackson have overcome the freeze response?

3. What other responses could Jackson's sympathetic nervous system have triggered?

4. What are the risks associated with a freeze response?

Physical effects of adrenalin on the body

Adrenaline is a hormone released by the adrenal glands that sit just above the kidneys. Adrenaline is released directly into the bloodstream so it can take only a second or two to have an effect. Its physical effects are:

- increased heart rate
- raised blood pressure
- increased blood flow to the muscles.

These physical responses prepare you to fight, flight or freeze. However, an adrenaline surge can have an effect on your perception of a situation as well. People who have had adrenaline surges have reported the following feelings:

- time slowing down
- tunnel vision
- reduced coordination
- lack of concentration
- difficulty thinking clearly.

Adrenaline can be a double-edged sword: it prepares your body for response, but it may harm your perceptions and decision-making abilities.

How to recognise symptoms of shock

If you have done first aid training you may recognise the term 'shock' as a sudden and dramatic loss of blood that can lead to unconsciousness and death. However, the term shock is used in other ways as well and it is important to recognise the differences.

In this context 'shock' is used to mean an acute stress reaction usually caused by a traumatic event such as an assault or bereavement. Figure 3.1 below contains some of the symptoms of an acute stress reaction.

Did you know?

An acute stress reaction can lead to Post-Traumatic Stress Disorder: a condition which leads to nightmares, inability to cope, depression, insomnia and mood swings.

Key term

Shock – an acute stress reaction usually caused by a traumatic event, such as an assault or bereavement.

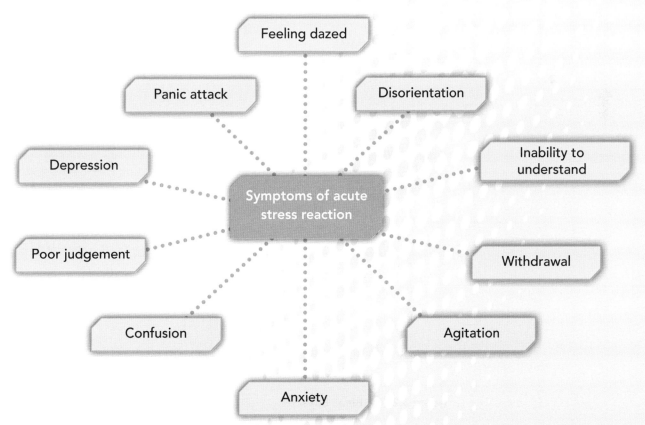

Figure 3.1: Some of the symptoms of acute stress reaction

2. Understand how to recognise, assess and reduce risk in conflict situations

Assessing the risks of conflict is a key part of your job in the security industry. A poorly judged response or action from you can lead to an escalation of conflict and potentially lead to violence.

2.1 Stages of escalation in conflict situations

The attitude–behaviour cycle

Your attitude affects your behaviour and this can create a vicious cycle: for example, if you have a bad attitude towards a certain group of people, you will deal with them more negatively, which will then lead them to be more negative with you and confirm your original attitude. This is visually explained in a diagram called the Betari Box (see Figure 3.2 below).

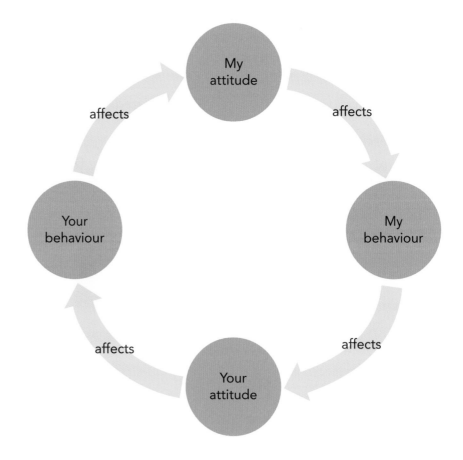

Figure 3.2: The Betari Box

Case study: Attitude–behaviour cycle

India is a CCTV control room operative in a large Scottish town.

"There are about four of us at any one time on the camera monitoring station. It's quite draining work looking at computer screens all day so it is important to take regular breaks, otherwise your eyes glaze over and you stop being observant. We are used to managing these breaks properly and covering for each other. We got a new manager recently and he has made it really clear he doesn't trust us. He spends his entire shift watching us to make sure we don't miss anything, timing our breaks and lunch to make sure we don't take one minute longer than we should. He has even checked our mailboxes to see if we are receiving personal e-mail at work.

As a result we've all become demotivated, we've stopped making decisions for ourselves and we ask permission for everything we do. It looks like we can't be bothered and have no initiative so it reinforces his poor impression of us. He doesn't realise it's his attitude that has caused this in the first place."

Over to you

1. How is the manager responsible for this situation?

2. How could the manager change his attitude and behaviour?

3. How could the team change their attitude and behaviour?

Escalation of threat

Keeping control of a conflict situation is essential, otherwise matters can escalate very quickly. The stages in escalation are as follows:

1. The situation creates frustration.

2. Frustration leads to anger.

3. Anger leads to aggression.

4. Aggression leads to violence.

You must take action to defuse the situation before it becomes violent.

Your actions

It is important to remember that your own actions and responses can escalate an already tense situation further. If you are unsympathetic or rude to a person who is already angry or distressed, you risk making the situation harder to resolve and escalating the risk of conflict and violence.

Activity: Threat escalation

You are working in a large town centre car park as a security officer. Without warning the payment machines break down simultaneously across the car park and the barriers become fixed in the down position. You are working solo and you have over 100 very unhappy motorists, including young families, who have been trapped in the car park for over an hour. The engineer has called to say he is delayed in traffic and will be at least another hour and you know that when the motorists find this out the situation may escalate.

1. What action could you take to calm the situation down?

2. What attitudes and behaviour should you avoid at all costs?

2.2 How to apply dynamic risk assessment in conflict situations

Key term

Dynamic risk assessment – a continuous assessment of risk in rapidly changing circumstances.

A **dynamic risk assessment** is a continuous assessment of risk in rapidly changing circumstances. It is a skill all good security operatives should have and practise on a daily basis. Table 3.3 below outlines several reasons why you might need to deploy this skill regularly.

Table 3.3: Dynamic risk assessment

Dynamic assessment	Description
Need to adapt to threats	You need to be able to adapt to different threats posed by people, places and objects. Potential risks in the security sector can come from anywhere and with very little warning. You need to be able to adapt quickly to new information picked up in situ and change your responses accordingly.
The reactionary gap	A close range interpersonal assault is almost impossible to prevent without injury as the space the attacker has to cross to assault you is so small that you do not have sufficient time to react. The reactionary gap is the space you need to leave between you and a potential assailant in order for you to have time to physically prevent an attack. A dynamic risk assessment will enable you to monitor this distance on a continuous basis to make sure your reactionary gap is not invaded, which could leave you vulnerable.
Early warning signs of potential aggression	Dynamic risk assessments can pick up on early warning signs that a situation is about to escalate (for example, non-verbal signals such as body language, changes to breathing rates and tone of voice) which means you have advance warning of trouble and can take suitable steps to calm the situation.
Danger signs of imminent anger and aggression	Dynamic assessment will enable you to take cues such as use of language, non-verbal signals and invasion of personal space to determine whether aggression is imminent. Dynamic assessment of the environment will enable you to determine if there are any actual and potential weapons which you need to remove or reposition in order to prevent violence developing.
Readiness to adapt your response depending on risk	A dynamic assessment enables you to make a decision on how to act, such as responding verbally, intervening, retreating or seeking help. Without the benefit of the assessment you wouldn't know which action to take in a given situation.

3. Understand how to communicate effectively in emotive situations and de-escalate conflict

Effective communication is essential in resolving conflict when it arises and preventing escalation. You need to consider how you communicate with others and what this says about your willingness to listen and empathise.

3.1 How to use non-verbal communication in emotive situations

The vast majority of our communication is done through non-verbal means such as body language, tone of voice and facial expression: only around 7% of what we communicate is the actual verbal message, so there is clearly scope for communication to be misunderstood and cause conflict.

Key term

Non-verbal communication – communicating through body language, tone of voice and facial expression.

How to signal non-aggression through non-verbal communication

If you are intending to signal that you have no aggressive intent towards someone then there are ways you can use your body and your tone of voice to de-escalate the situation (see Table 3.4 below).

Table 3.4: Non-verbal cues

Non-verbal cue	Explanation
Posture	You should keep your posture alert, but relaxed. Your shoulders should be down and you should evenly distribute your weight across both feet in an easy stance. This enables you to give the impression of being calm and approachable if someone has a problem, but has the advantage that you could switch posture to deal with an attack very quickly.
Positioning	You should position yourself in the right proxemic zone (see page 124) for the situation and be wary of intimidating someone with your size by being too far into their personal space – this can be viewed as a very aggressive move. However keeping an extreme distance from a person may hinder you in solving their concern or complaint – use your judgement effectively.
Movements	Your movements should be well telegraphed and relaxed, not quick and jerky. Do not fidget as this can indicate you are nervous and uncertain.
Hand gestures	Open-handed gestures show that you are not about to become aggressive and also show that you are not armed. Uncrossing your arms indicates a willingness to be open and professional. Avoid pointing, finger wagging and clenched fists.
Voice pitch	Your pitch should be your normal tone. When conflict is escalating it can sometimes pay to slow your speech and lower your tone. Do not shout, use sarcasm, tut, sigh or demonstrate you are angry or annoyed with any non-verbal signals.

Open-handed gestures show that you are not about to become aggressive.

Key term

Proxemic zone – spatial boundary determined by your social closeness to another person.

Activity: Proxemic zones

We are normally acutely aware of our spatial boundaries. Choose a partner from your training class or your workplace that you do not know well and try this exercise. Stand 12 feet apart facing each other and move in a step at a time. At what point does it become too uncomfortable to you to move closer? This is the key boundary you need to keep in mind if you are going to avoid conflict with others by entering their space – or be aware that you might demonstrate a negative reaction if someone invades yours.

Remember as well that your appearance is a key part of your non-verbal communication, so make sure that you are clean and well-presented. If you are required to wear a uniform, make sure it is well-kept and pressed. A dirty or unkempt appearance can have a very negative impression on people. Also be aware that excessive jewellery can look intimidating as well as being a health and safety hazard if you are involved in a physical intervention.

Proxemic zones

Proxemic zones are our spatial boundaries; they are a measure of how close we allow someone to us. This concept was developed by communication researcher Edward Hall, who argued that all of us have four proxemic zones (see Figure 3.3 below):

- **Intimate** – the zone where you allow those who you have a close relationship with, such as family or partners
- **Personal** – the distance maintained between friends
- **Social** – the distance maintained between business colleagues
- **Public** – the distance maintained between strangers.

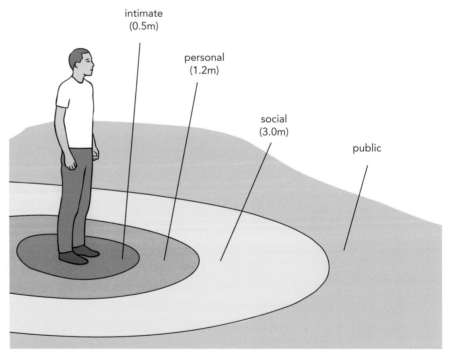

Figure 3.3: Proxemic zones

Most people keep these distances without even realising it. When someone comes too close to us and breaks a proxemic boundary it can make us feel uncomfortable. If someone invades your space or you are forced in a crowded environment to invade theirs, be aware that conflict might follow.

3.2 How to overcome communication barriers

Communication is not as straightforward as simply speaking to someone, putting up a sign or instructing someone to do what you want them to do. Communication is complex and there can be many barriers to getting your message across to your customers, clients and the public.

Types of communication barrier and ways to overcome them

The following are some barriers to communication:

- **Physical** – sometimes there are physical barriers to effective communication such as doors, windows, other people, site noise and loud music. One of the most effective ways of removing this type of barrier is by moving to a quieter or more accessible location so that both parties can hear each other freely.

- **Attitudinal** – people can have very negative attitudes to certain information or requests you need to give them and it can be hard to communicate past these barriers. You can try and overcome this by making sure you restate your message so misunderstandings do not take place and remaining assertive so that the person realises the message or request is going to be consistent and they cannot influence you to change by their poor attitude.

- **Emotional** – if people are upset they will have emotional barriers which may make communicating with them very difficult. You can overcome this by defusing the situation and empathising with them. If a person can be supported to remain calm you have a better chance of effective communication.

- **Linguistic** – some security staff, particularly at airports, travel venues and large cities, are likely to come across individuals for whom English is not their first language or who have an accent which is difficult to understand. Equally as a security operative you need to be sure that your own standard of English and accent can be understood by others. You can overcome some of these barriers by re-phrasing and repeating messages, slowing your speech and pronouncing your words clearly, not using local slang or industry jargon, using gestures to make yourself understood and using an interpreter if required. You should also use active listening as discussed in section 3.4 to assist with communication and understanding.

Did you know?

Proxemic zones are culturally defined. The ones described in Figure 3.3 are for Western Europeans and North Americans. In South America and the Middle East much closer proxemic distances are used for interaction and in the far East and Asia much greater distances are used.

3.3 Differences between assertiveness and aggression

Assertiveness is about recognising that your needs and wants are as important as the needs and wants of others (see Figure 3.4). Aggressive behaviour can stem from thinking that your needs and wants are more important than those of others and being prepared to shout down those who challenge that perception (see Figure 3.5).

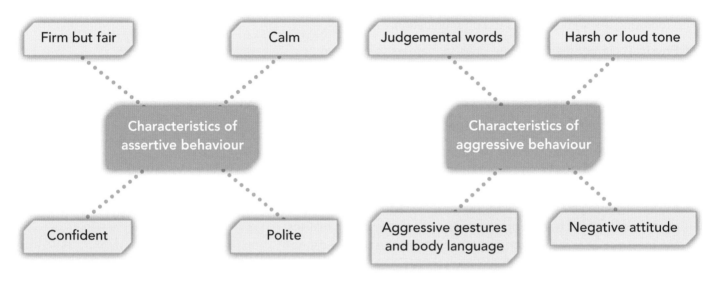

Figure 3.4: Characteristics of assertive behaviour

Figure 3.5: Characteristics of aggressive behaviour

3.4 Ways of defusing emotive conflict situations

Use of non-verbal communication to signal non-aggression

This has already been covered in section 3.1 Table 3.4 on page 123.

Maintaining self-control

The security industry is stressful and pressurised. You will be dealing with conflict on a regular basis and you will be provoked with insults, aggression, violence and verbal abuse. You must ensure you maintain your self-control and keep your temper. You are working with the public in a professional environment where your conduct and interaction with customers can directly affect how much money is made by your employer and how good their reputation is in the industry. Remain respectful and polite at all time, never take conflict personally and never lose your temper.

Being positive and assertive

Having a positive attitude in the workplace can make your shift easier and more rewarding, not just for you, but also for your colleagues and your customers. Don't be negative and don't make assumptions about the people you come into contact with; Section 2.1 looked at how your attitude influences your behaviour, which in turn influences the attitude and behaviour of others. By remaining positive you are more likely to have positive interactions with others.

Being assertive means respecting yourself and others. It is about standing up for your needs in a way that respects and acknowledges that others have needs too. This approach makes compromise and win–win situations more likely to be successful and will reduce the escalation of conflict.

Empathy and active listening

Empathy is discussed in detail in section 4.1 of this unit, see page 131.

Active listening is an important skill for any security operative. Figure 3.6 below outlines some of the key skills you need for active listening. It involves listening carefully to what is being said in a non-biased and judgement-free way. You should not interrupt, finish people's sentences or jump to conclusions about the point they are trying to get across. Ensure people have finished what they are saying before you make a response and repeat back to them what you have heard so that you can be sure you have understood. If you don't understand what point they are trying to make then don't be afraid to ask questions to clarify: it is better to ask questions than take the wrong course of action because you didn't understand.

Did you know?

Remember that when people are drunk or frightened it may be more difficult to understand them. They may also say things that they don't mean or will regret later – don't take any insults or criticism personally.

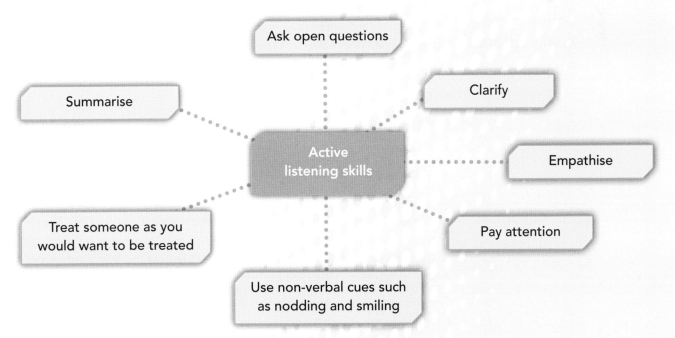

Figure 3.6: How to be an active listener

3.5 Appropriate approaches to take when confronting unacceptable behaviour

It is inevitable that you will have to deal with unacceptable behaviour while working in the security industry whether in entertainment venues, shopping centres or on commercial and business premises. The approach you take to the behaviour can often dictate the outcome.

Following appropriate policy and procedures

It is essential that you know the policy and procedures that your employer has in place for dealing with conflict situations and that you follow them. They are not only a protective mechanism for the public, they also exist to protect you. By following them you can explain to the public why a particular behaviour is not allowed and why they need to stop. They will be more likely to comply with a request you make if they understand the reasons you are making it.

Being proactive

In many security situations it is better to head off less serious behaviour by being proactive with a friendly or quiet word to those involved than to stand back and wait for the situation to escalate into a more serious conflict. If you intervene early you can prevent conflict from forming and save yourself time and trouble down the line. It is better to be proactive and prevent trouble than react to trouble.

Using assertive language and behaviour

The REACT mnemonic is used in the door supervision sector in particular to guide how to challenge unacceptable behaviour in an assertive, but non-aggressive manner (see Figure 3.7 on page 129 for an example). It can easily be adapted to suit the rest of the security industry.

- **R**equest
- **E**xplain
- **A**ppeal
- **C**onfirm
- **T**ake action

The first stage is to ask a member of the public to comply with a *request*, such as to leave the premises, show their identification, sign in or explain what they are doing. The vast majority of people will respond to the request and do as you have asked. However there will always be a small proportion who do not.

The second stage is to *explain* to the member of the public why you have made the request and explain the importance of complying, such as health and safety, company policy or legal requirements.

If the individual still does not comply then you should *appeal* to them to do what they are being asked and explain what action will be taken against them, such as being removed from the premises or the police being called.

If the individual still does not comply you should *confirm* they understand what they have been told and that they understand the consequences of their refusal. It is also good practice at this point to give the person one more chance to comply.

The final stage is to *take action*. For door supervisors and some security staff this might mean the ejection of a person from the premises, for other security staff it may mean a call to the police. If you are responsible for ejecting a person from the premises ensure you do not do so alone. Not only is it easier to work as a team with colleagues to do this, but you also have witnesses to testify that minimum force was used should your angry customer or site trespasser decide to make a complaint about you.

Throughout the experience your behaviour should be calm and professional and your language assertive in tone.

3.6 How to work with colleagues to de-escalate conflict situations

Positioning of staff members in a confrontation

Depending on which part of the security industry you work in you may be able to deploy other members of staff to assist in a confrontation situation. For door supervisors this is usually relatively straightforward as it is likely you will be working in close proximity to your colleagues. Security staff in other venues may have more difficulty with this, particularly if you are a lone worker, conduct remote patrols or are part of a small team on a large site. It is important that if you are working with a colleague you have established in advance the positioning you will take. Usually the member of staff not actively involved in the confrontation will be close enough to respond if required, ideally within 12 feet and offset to the side so they are visible as a deterrent. This will be covered in more detail in Unit 4 Physical intervention.

Request – 'Please can you leave the premises/show your identification/sign in/explain what you are doing?'

↓

Explain – 'I need to see your identification because it's company policy'

↓

Appeal – 'Please will you show me your identification? If you do not I will have to ask you to leave the premises'

↓

Confirm – 'Do you understand what I'm asking you to do? Please can you show me your identification?'

↓

Take action – Ask a colleague for assistance, then ask the customer to leave the premises. If they refuse to do so, you should escort them off the premises with minimum force.

Figure 3.7: Example of REACT being used

It is likely you will be working in close proximity to your colleagues.

Handing over to, or taking control from, a colleague in a confrontation

Conflict situations can make people very angry and upset and, although you are a professional, there will be times when you are extremely angry with a member of the public. This makes the situation very difficult, as it can be hard to overcome the anger in order to solve the conflict you are presented with. In situations such as this it can be a real benefit to hand over to a colleague who is calm and can take the situation from there. You can then take a step back and calm down and the person you are dealing with might appreciate a change of personnel meaning that the conflict may be resolved more quickly. Your colleagues may also require you to step in and assist when they are struggling with anger and you should be prepared to do so in a supportive way.

For some security staff, particularly those individuals who work in door supervision, dealing with angry and aggressive behaviour can be a daily occurrence. You need to overlook the outward signs of anger and upset in order to see what the real issues are.

3.7 Importance of positioning and exit routes

How you position yourself in a conflict situation is very important for your own safety and the safety of others.

Importance of leaving potential aggressors with an exit route

Your aim in each conflict situation is to resolve, de-escalate or defuse the conflict and one of the ways you can do this is by making sure that any potential aggressor can turn around and walk away freely. Do not position yourself to block their exit: if you prevent them from walking away the conflict is very likely to escalate.

Importance of having own exit route available

It is very important to your own safety that you also have a clear exit route. Consider your surroundings and position yourself so that you can get away if you are attacked or feel threatened. If a door is nearby, is it open or closed? Is it locked? Can you retreat on foot to a secure room until the police arrive if you are a lone worker on a remote site?

4. Understand how to develop and use problem-solving strategies for resolving conflict

4.1 Importance of viewing the situation from the customer's perspective

Customers have a right to have their issues and complaints heard. Taking on board customer feedback and responding to it can make businesses more successful and more competitive in an increasingly difficult economic environment. As a member of the security staff of an organisation you might be the first contact a customer has with an organisation if they have a complaint or problem so it is essential you deal with it professionally.

The value of empathy

Empathy is about understanding and identifying with how someone feels about a situation. It is a really important tool that security personnel can use to prevent conflict, defuse conflict and understand the conflict situation better. Empathy for a person does not change what the outcome will be for them, but it will make them feel better about that outcome. For example you might find a drunken customer is causing problems for the bar staff and upsetting other customers in a large wine bar. When you approach him about his behaviour he might explain that he has just found his girlfriend and his best friend in a compromising situation – you may empathise with his position, but it doesn't change the fact that if he doesn't change his behaviour you will have to ask him to leave the bar.

A show of empathy can create trust and defuse a situation. If a member of the public is angry and upset then showing them you understand and empathise might be all that is required to divert the conflict.

Ways of showing empathy

In order to reduce conflict by showing empathy there are several things that you can do:

1. Give the person your full attention.

2. Maintain eye contact with them, but do not stare as this can be confrontational.

3. Ask appropriate questions to show you have understood.

4. Share a story about when something similar happened to you so the customer knows you have gone through a similar experience.

> **Key term**
>
> Empathy – understanding and identifying with how someone feels about a situation. It is about putting yourself in their shoes and considering how they feel.

5. Be respectful and treat others as you would want to be treated.

6. Be a good listener.

7. Don't finish their sentences or interrupt them.

8. Don't fidget or show impatience.

Remember it is better to spend ten minutes showing a customer empathy than three hours filling in the paperwork and dealing with the police after a physical intervention.

4.2 Strategies for solving problems

Once you have defused the anger in a situation you still have to solve the underlying problem that caused the situation in the first place. There are several techniques that can make this easier:

- **Build rapport** – rapport is the principle of mutual trust and understanding between people. If you can build a rapport with someone this can lead to open and honest communication about a problem and lead to a quicker resolution.

- **Find common ground** – rather than concentrating on the issues where you disagree with someone, try finding the points where you do agree and work from there. It is a more positive approach and can lead to a quicker resolution.

- **Agree a way forward** – rather than looking at what has already happened in the conflict, look at where you want to go and agree a way to reach it. This provides a fresh start to the problem.

Table 3.5 below outlines some strategies you can use to solve problems.

Table 3.5: Negotiation strategies that can be used to help solve problems

Negotiation strategy	Explanation
Stating expectations	As explained in section 1.5, stating what you expect from the people you are dealing with can be a sound negotiating tool in reducing conflict. If people know what the boundaries are and the consequences of breaking these boundaries you are less likely to experience conflict.
Giving reasons	As explained in section 3.5 under the REACT mnemonic, providing people with a reason for your actions, such as legal responsibilities, company policies or health and safety law, can reduce conflict or de-escalate it if it has already begun.
Offering alternatives	Providing a range of alternatives to customers allows them to choose the option that best suits them. For example if a female refuses a search from a male officer, offer the alternative of a female officer to search – this would be good practice in any case.
Applying pressure	Pressure can be subtly applied to individuals in order to resolve conflict: discussing the consequences (such as police involvement) of continued aggressive or poor behaviour can make individuals reconsider their approach.

Table 3.5 (cont.)

Negotiation strategies	Explanation
Offering incentives	You can offer an incentive to individuals to avoid conflict, particularly if you feel their grounds for conflict are justified. This could be free tickets, free refreshments or agreeing to organise a meeting with a more senior member of staff so an individual's concerns can be heard at a higher level, depending on your organisation.
Compromising	A compromise is a solution to the conflict which is not ideal to either party, but is an acceptable middle ground. It averts and reduces conflict by ensuring each party receives at least part of what they require.

4.3 Win–win approaches to conflict situations

The concept of 'win–win'

A win–win approach is a negotiated agreement where both parties are satisfied with the outcome of the conflict situation. In conflict situations we often find ourselves in a knee-jerk reaction of 'do it my way'. Is there a way you could both come out of the situation with what you want? If so, how could you go about it?

Be fair and open but firm in a conflict situation.

Activity: Win–win

You are the security manager for a large entertainment venue. During a gig you are notified of a conflict situation developing and you head over to find out what the issue is. Around 10 people are shouting at the event stewards and around 50 more are gathered behind them. You calm the situation down and ask what the problem is. The issue is that people have been placed behind large pillars by the event stewards in an area of the venue that has poor visibility of the stage. You know that those seats aren't normally sold for small gigs like this one and you know the people are not getting their money's worth. Consider the following options:

A You ignore the reasons why they are angry and tell the people to sit down or they will be removed from the venue.

B You empathise with the crowd but tell them there is nothing you can do about it and ask them to retake their seats.

C You publicly discipline the stewards and have a fresh row of seating set up in front of the stage for the people to move to – it's crowded, but you just hope they will fit.

D You listen to the concerns and understand the situation and then liaise with the entertainment manager to negotiate a choice of three options for the crowd: either a refund, free tickets for the next time the band play the venue, or they can slot into the free seats elsewhere in the venue with an unrestricted view.

1. Explain the advantages and disadvantages of each approach.
2. Are any of these options a win–win solution?

Benefit of win–win approaches

Win–win approaches to conflict management have the following advantages:

- Everyone is satisfied with the outcome.

- Reduced risk of conflict escalation and aggression.

- Minimal negative feelings.

- Positive publicity.

- The public and staff are safer.

- Reduced costs to the employer in terms of injuries and negative press.

5. Understand good practice to follow after conflict situations

Conflict situations can be frightening and intimidating even for highly experienced security and door staff, so it is important to know how to seek support, reflect on your reactions and share good practice so that you are better able to deal with a similar situation if it arises again.

5.1 Importance of accessing help and support following an incident

As you will have seen in section 1.6, the human body can have a range of responses to conflict situations such as acute stress responses, shock and even post-traumatic stress disorder (PTSD) so it is crucial to know who to seek support from if you need it or offer support to affected colleagues.

Sources of help and support

You have a variety of sources of support available to you such as:

- colleagues

- management

- counsellors

- friends

- family

- mentors.

Each of these groups will be able to support you in different ways depending on your needs. Security staff often find colleagues a huge source of support since they have dealt with similar situations and gone through similar emotions. However if the problem is more severe it is better to turn to professional and impartial support such as a counsellor or psychologist. Your G.P. can make a referral or you can pay privately for the service.

Value of accessing help and support

You should never be concerned or ashamed of seeking help and support. Appropriate support can help you cope more effectively, especially if you are returning to work or have to carry on working after an incident. It can provide reassurance that you acted appropriately and put your mind at ease and it can help bring you out of a shocked state.

5.2 Importance of reflecting on and learning from conflict situations

Reflecting is considering one's own experiences in applying knowledge to practice. In essence it is learning from experience. Reflecting is extremely important to new security and door staff as it will help you identify how you can review and improve your own practice. It is equally important to experienced security and door staff in the context of continuous improvement.

Value of reflecting and learning from conflict

Reflecting on how you acted in a particular situation allows you to think objectively about what happened and consider what you might do differently next time. It provides you with the opportunity to:

- **recognise trends.** Is this something that happens often? Is your response always the same? What are the causes and can you do anything about them?

- **respond better in future.** You may consider your response and think that you could have done something better or avoided doing something poorly. Reflecting will give you the chance to avoid these responses next time.

- **identify preventative measures.** By reflecting on the patterns in the conflict around you it may be that you can come up with some preventative measures and reduce the overall level of conflict that you deal with.

Benefits of reflection

Reflection has several benefits for you:

- It can improve the quality of your work.

- It enables you to view events objectively.

- It enables you to transfer what you do well to other similar situations.

> **Key term**
>
> Reflection – considering one's own experiences in applying knowledge to practice. It is the process of thinking about what you did, where it went right or wrong and deciding how you will change your behaviour the next time a similar situation occurs.

- It improves your professional judgement.
- It helps you identify your staff development needs.
- It helps you identify where you need to make changes or improvements.
- You can learn from the experience of others.
- It makes you a more confident and competent door supervisor and security officer.

For your customers:

- You will have a better understanding of their reactions to stress and conflict.
- They will be safer.
- Continuous improvement in the quality of the security service they receive.

For your colleagues and organisation:

- Shared sense of common purpose and responsibility for the safety of all customers.
- Higher levels of shared professional expertise.
- Increased understanding of security policies and best practice.
- Reduced fear of difficult situations.
- Increasing levels of professional support and communication.

5.3 Importance of sharing good practice

Sharing good practice enables those who are more experienced in the security sector to pass on their considerable skills and knowledge to new operatives and allows new members of the team to bring a fresh and up-to-date approach to security matters. It is a mutually beneficial sharing of ideas.

Why staff should contribute

Sharing good practice allows you to:

- know the value of first hand experience. A colleague may have been through a situation you have yet to encounter. Hearing about it first hand might help you prepare more effectively for when the situation happens to you.
- share expertise. No one person can know everything about a job. Sharing expertise allows you access to information and experience you would not otherwise receive.

- facilitate the use of common approaches. It is important that all security operatives work consistently at a venue to ensure there are no weak links or loopholes where conflict could happen.

- respond to changing circumstances. The security industry and the types of situations it deals with can change very rapidly. Sharing good practice enables you to keep abreast of the latest developments.

- influence procedures. Sharing good practice can empower you to suggest changes to outdated or inaccurate security procedures.

5.4 Importance of contributing to solutions to recurring problems

If there is a recurring problem in your workplace it is your responsibility to help to come up with a viable solution. Your colleagues and manager will welcome your constructive involvement and it will have larger benefits for you and your organisation, as Table 3.6 outlines.

Table 3.6: Benefits of contributing

Benefits of contributing	Explanation
Safer working environment	Staff and customers will be safer and enjoy their work/leisure time more if recurring security problems are dealt with satisfactorily.
Reduced stress	One less problem for you to deal with during your shift is one less source of stress for you, your customers and your employer.
Improved customer experience	Customers do not enjoy spending their leisure time in an environment where conflict might happen or they don't feel safe. They will have a better experience if problems are solved and this means that they will feel more relaxed, spend more money, come to your venue more frequently and consequently improve the financial health of the organisation.

Just checking

1. Why is it important to know your company's policy on conflict management?

2. Name two factors that can trigger an angry response in another person.

3. Name two factors that can inhibit an angry response in another person.

4. How can unrealistic expectations from customers lead to conflict?

5. Explain the fight, flight and freeze responses.

6. What is the effect of adrenaline on the body?

7. Explain the Betari box cycle.

8. What is a dynamic risk assessment?

9. Describe the reactionary gap.

10. What are the differences between assertiveness and aggression?

11. How does empathy reduce conflict escalation?

12. What is the win–win approach to conflict?

13. What are the benefits of sharing good practice?

14. What are the benefits of reflection on conflict situations?

15. Where would you seek help to overcome the aftermath of a conflict situation?

Jason Weston
Security Team Manager at a medium-sized venue

Conflict can happen really quickly in this kind of work: one minute you can be laughing and joking with the customers and the next you have a fight break out or have someone shouting the odds. Making sure the customers know what to expect and giving them correct information is a key factor in reducing conflict. We recently took on a new officer who was freshly qualified, and I'd sent him out to monitor the queues building up outside the venue. The weather wasn't too good and the new officer in his warm high-visibility waterproofs and fleece was laughing at some of the little dresses the female customers were wearing and generally making fun of them by telling them they would be standing in the cold and rain for hours while the band got set up.

The customers were furious and a huge row erupted. I pulled him in from queue duty and put one of my more experienced staff out there to calm things down and get people moving into the club. I gave my new staff member a real dressing down and reminded him that if he couldn't treat our customers with courtesy and respect and provide them with accurate information his stint as an officer with my team would be very short. Despite being trained he didn't have the empathy to understand how other people would feel about his behaviour – it was a classic example of someone with 'all the gear, but no idea'!

Over to you

1. Why do you think the customers were angry?
2. What were the key issues with the new officer's behaviour?
3. Was Jason's response after the incident an appropriate one?
4. What would you have done if you were Jason?

4 Physical intervention skills for the private security industry

Expert training in physical intervention is an important part of the skills required for a professional door supervisor or anyone working in the security industry.

It is important for you to be knowledgeable, not only about the actual procedures, moves and techniques associated with physical intervention but also about what the law stipulates to be 'reasonable force'. The use of lawful force, however minimal, should always be regarded as an absolute last resort. Interpersonal skills are very important to defuse a situation and the focus should always be on preventative action.

In this unit you will learn about how to reduce the risks when physical intervention is used, dynamic risk assessment, risk factors and responsibilities following a physical intervention.

The aim of this unit is to fully equip you with all the necessary skills and knowledge required to engage in acts of physical intervention safely and confidently within the confines of the law, whenever the necessity arises. This unit builds on the knowledge covered in previous units and must not be taken until Units 1, 2 and 3 have been taught.

Learning outcomes

After completing this unit you should:

1. understand physical interventions and the legal/professional implications of their use
2. understand how to reduce the risk of harm when physical intervention skills are used
3. be able to use non-aggressive physical skills to protect yourself and others from assault*
4. be able to use non-pain-related standing holding and escorting techniques, including non-restrictive and restrictive skills*
5. understand good practice to follow after physical intervention.

*Learning outcomes 3 and 4 will be covered in a practical session with your trainer and are not covered as part of this book.

Security alert!

Physical intervention skills

This unit is designed to teach you simple holding, restraint, guiding and break-away techniques that can be used as a last resort in conflict management to prevent situations from escalating and bring them under control. You do not need any previous training to be able to learn these techniques.

On your own, or in pairs, ask yourself the following questions:

- Do you feel that physical intervention is needed in the role of a door supervisor?

- When do you think that physical intervention should be used?

- What do you think you will find challenging about using physical intervention techniques?

1. Understand physical interventions and the legal/professional implications of their use

1.1 The differences between defensive physical skills and physical intervention

Physical intervention means to become physically involved in a situation in order to resolve conflict, avoid assault and to prevent the situation from getting any worse.

As a door supervisor, you will need to develop interpersonal communication skills which will enable you to assess any given situation and defuse potentially violent situations before they develop.

However, at some point in your career, it will undoubtedly be necessary for you to use your physical intervention skills to:

- resolve conflict

- avoid assault to yourself and others around you

- maintain a safe and secure environment.

Under no circumstances should physical intervention be mistaken for violent acts of aggression. The act of physically intervening should also

Key term

Physical intervention – the direct or indirect use of force (bodily, physical, mechanical) to limit another person's movement.

not be viewed as, or be an excuse for, acting with violence. The physical force used should always be non-aggressive and non-violent and only be used as an absolute last resort. Remember, any type of physical intervention is an assault unless you can justify its use.

Defensive physical skills are a range of skills which, when implemented, will protect you or someone else from assault or injury. For example, defensive physical skills can be break-away techniques. If a customer physically grabs you, then you may choose to use a defensive break-away technique to protect yourself and others from injury and harm.

Key term

Defensive physical skills – a range of skills which you can use to protect yourself or another person from assault or injury.

What would you do?: Using indirect defensive physical skills

You are asking a customer, who is under the influence of drugs or alcohol, to leave the premises. You use conflict management techniques such as explaining why you are asking them to leave and gesturing with extended arms and open palms towards the direction of the exit (known as a shepherding and guiding technique). The customer grabs your wrist. In response you ask them to let go in a calm and measured tone. If this fails, you then use defensive physical skills to break-away and step back from the customer's grip. You continue to use conflict management techniques to calmly reassure and speak to the customer.

What would you do?: Using direct physical intervention skills

You have asked the customer in the previous scenario to leave the premises. They have grabbed your wrist and you have used defensive physical skills to break-away from their hold. The customer then escalates the situation by invading your personal space, using abuse focused on you personally and using aggressive body language. You assess the situation and call for back up. A colleague arrives and you decide to use practised techniques of physical intervention because you believe the customer is not going to leave on their own. They are not responding to reasonable requests to leave and are becoming a potential hazard to themselves and to others. Physical intervention techniques may be reasonable to use to escort the customer from the premises. They should be used in a way that will safely remove the customer without causing pain and injury to the customer, to others or to yourself.

Practise using the shepherding technique to guide and direct customers.

1.2 The differences between non–restrictive and restrictive intervention

Physical interventions can be defined in two broad categories:

- Non-restrictive (associated with a lower level of risk)
- Restrictive (where a higher level of risk is present).

Non-restrictive intervention is where the person is free to move or to leave of their own accord. An example of non-restrictive intervention is the shepherding and guiding technique discussed in the defensive physical skills on the previous page.

By contrast, restrictive intervention is designed to prevent, impede or restrict mobility and movement. An example of restrictive intervention is the technique explained on the previous page where you use physical intervention techniques to remove someone from the premises. The main difference between non-restrictive and restrictive physical intervention is the level of the intervention and the degree of force applied.

Restrictive intervention can be divided into highly restrictive or low-level restrictive. Highly restrictive intervention is one that severely limits the movement or freedom of an individual (for example, where two door supervisors restrain one arm each). Low-level restrictive intervention is one that limits or contains the movement and freedom of an individual with lower levels of force (for example, one door supervisor using forearm support).

Key terms

Non-restrictive intervention – the person is free to move of their own accord.

Restrictive intervention – the person's movement is limited.

Restrictive physical interventions may be planned or unplanned (emergency). Planned restrictive physical interventions are usually thought out in advance when assessing likely risks in a door supervisor's role. They are responses that are planned ahead of time in response to anticipated incidents and clearly defined behaviours.

In exceptional circumstances, there may be a need for emergency or unplanned interventions. The emergency use of restrictive physical interventions may be required when people behave in unforeseen ways. This could be as a result of taking drugs or drinking alcohol or mental health issues. Even in an emergency, the use of force must be reasonable, in terms of intensity and duration, and the specific circumstances of the situation.

Before using restrictive physical intervention in an emergency, you should be confident that the possible negative outcomes (injury or distress) will be less severe than the adverse consequences of not intervening.

In general, if someone is at immediate risk of injury from a person's actions or if serious damage is likely to occur, then it might be necessary to intervene using restrictive physical intervention. Care should always be taken to avoid the use of excessive force and to prevent injury to yourself and to the person you are restraining.

Case study: Derek, physical intervention in an emergency

I have seen some people go from being reasonable one minute to responding emotionally or aggressively the next. A customer may seem to act normally and be in control, but the next minute they may be triggered by something. In my experience it could be anything but a common trigger may be seeing a person in uniform. Uniforms represent power and authority to some people and they may respond negatively to this association. It could recall a previous bad experience. If a person is suffering from a mental illness or a head injury or is under the influence of drugs or alcohol they may react spontaneously and aggressively to the perceived threat of a person in uniform. As a door supervisor you may need to respond immediately to prevent the customer from hurting themselves and others or causing damage to property. There may not be the time or opportunity to apply conflict management techniques and the only way to bring a situation under control is to restrain the customer and to follow up with communication skills throughout the restraint.

Over to you

1. List as many factors as you can that could trigger an emotional or aggressive response in a club.

2. What are the benefits of using restraining techniques if an aggressive customer does not respond to your requests.

3. Why is it important to use your communication skills when restraining a customer?

How can good conflict-management techniques reduce the need for physical intervention?

Key terms

Primary controls – preventative actions to stop incidents in the first place.

Secondary control – an early response to incidents as they develop.

Most venues display posters (like this one) which clearly outline the venue's policy towards providing proof of age.

1.3 Positive alternatives to physical intervention

Door supervisors may find themselves in situations where they are harassed or facing aggression or physical violence. Using force to resolve conflict should always be a last resort. Receiving physical intervention training does not mean you have licence to use force. It means using a controlled and professional response to situations in which conflict may arise. If violence and aggression are met with violence and aggression, the situation will escalate.

Unit 3 covers conflict management and how clear and effective communication can prevent situations escalating and provide a positive alternative to physical intervention. Once good conflict management techniques have been applied, aggression and, therefore, the necessity for physical intervention, is reduced and may disappear altogether. Conflict management must always be the first choice to defuse any situation. You can usually talk your way out of trouble and calm situations that are becoming heated. By using appropriate communication skills and body language, you can usually talk customers round and show them that conflict is not the best option.

Conflict management uses both primary and secondary controls. **Primary controls** are preventative actions to stop incidents in the first place. A **secondary control** is an early response to incidents as they develop.

Primary controls are essential to reduce the potential for conflict in a venue or workplace. As a door supervisor, it is important to be aware of what situations and environments may have the potential to cause conflict and to avoid them. Being aware of procedures, times and places that can trigger a potentially problematic situation, and being prepared to deal with them, will give you the ability to act rationally, decisively and professionally. Building up a good rapport with regular customers so that there is mutual respect can be one of the most important primary controls that you can develop.

Other primary controls may include:

- **queuing to get into a venue** – Access procedures such as searching and checking for proof of age and identity can be time consuming and lead to a large queue for people to get into a venue. Often admittance procedures take place at night with unfavourable weather conditions. Frustration can lead to aggression.

- **refusing entry** – It may be necessary, for a number of reasons, for you to refuse entry to an individual and such a situation may escalate negatively.

- **closing time** – Although the vast majority of visitors to the venue willingly comply with policies and procedures including closing time, a minority may prove to be difficult, so effective and positive communication skills are essential in order to prevent any situation from escalating.

Activity: Primary controls

You are a door supervisor in front of a busy nightclub in the town centre. It is Saturday night and the club is very busy with a queue of at least 60 people waiting to get in. The next customer in the queue appears to have consumed too much alcohol before coming to your venue. The Licensing Act stipulates that you cannot serve alcohol to someone if they are drunk, so it's good practice to refuse them entry to licensed premises. Someone who is under the influence of alcohol could also cause health and safety issues – they may slip and hurt themselves or others or could potentially be aggressive and cause conflict.

1. What potential problems are going to occur as a result of the delays while you are dealing with this issue?

2. What could you have done earlier to ensure you did not have this problem at the club entrance? Think about assessing people in the queue before they get to the door or the number of staff who are on the door.

A primary control could be following correct safety and security policies and procedures and working practices. It can also involve using equipment and technology such as radios or CCTV.

The security organisation you work for should have clear and concise risk-reduction procedures. These should include:

- set standards of behaviour, procedures and policies
- details of when and how to respond to situations
- procedures for preventing the entrance of known and persistent offenders
- a review procedure where staff can learn and reflect upon incidents that have occurred that night.

Other necessary primary control procedures to deter and minimise situations typically include:

- using CCTV in known 'trouble' spots
- well-positioned and highly visible staff as a deterrent
- using signs detailing the negative consequences of violent and anti-social behaviour
- effective team communication
- ensuring police involvement with more serious offences
- ensuring that certain areas don't become overcrowded

Did you know?

The Pubwatch scheme has been running in the UK for over 40 years. It is a way for the licensed premises in an area to agree to a joint approach to alcohol-related crime and anti-social behaviour. Typically, they refuse to serve people who have a history of causing problems. Currently there are more than 400 schemes, each involving between 5 and 200 licensed premises.

Pubwatch also operates radio systems to enable communication between CCTV, police and licensed venues.

For a link to the Pubwatch site, please visit www.pearsonhotlinks. co.uk

- joining a Pubwatch scheme or using radios that link in with town-centre CCTV, the police and other pubs and clubs in the area.

A secondary control is a response to prevent a situation escalating and these techniques are discussed in more depth in Unit 3 Conflict management. It is important to remember that as a door supervisor, you may be working in loud, fast-paced and hot environments where verbal communication is often difficult. Words and meanings can be misunderstood and misinterpreted leading to frustration and possibly aggression and violence. However, by staying calm and in control, using effective communication skills and an open and positive stance, you can prevent a situation from developing and escalating and reduce the need for physical intervention.

Through the combined use of well-thought-out and planned primary controls and excellent use of secondary controls and training, physical intervention becomes an absolute last resort.

1.4 The importance of using physical intervention only as a last resort

In situations of potential conflict, it is important to stay calm and in control, avoid confrontation and de-escalate any potential conflict. There are many techniques that you can employ to defuse a situation rather than physical intervention. It is very important to remember that inappropriate use of physical restraint may give rise to criminal charges. It is also a criminal offence to threaten the use of force.

Physical intervention should always be a last resort.

Restrictive physical restraint or intervention should be used as a last resort and should also be part of a general behaviour management strategy. Physical intervention should be used as a last resort because:

- it can cause increased risk of harm and injury to staff and customers

- it increases the potential of allegations against staff of the use of unnecessary force

- it could lead to loss of a venue's licence or a door supervisor's job.

Restrictive physical restraint or intervention should only be used when:

- other, less-intrusive strategies have been tried and found to be unsuccessful

- the risks of not using an emergency intervention are outweighed by the need to intervene

- it is perceived that a customer or other person is in danger or there is a serious risk to property with a consequent risk to people's safety

- it is not possible or appropriate to withdraw.

1.5 Legal and professional implications relating to the use of physical intervention

Legislation surrounding the use of physical intervention and the use of force varies considerably and emphasis is placed upon the actual event itself and the outcome.

Generally speaking, the use of force by an individual against another individual could be classed as unlawful assault – *unless it can be justified*.

Activity: Use of reasonable force

A customer in a night club becomes verbally aggressive with door staff. The door supervisor talks calmly to the customer and defuses the situation. The customer goes away and continues to drink alcohol. Later on in the evening, the customer re-approaches the door supervisor in an aggressive and threatening way and is escorted out of the venue and asked to leave. The customer then returns, carrying a knuckle duster (an offensive weapon) and is threatening and abusive. The door supervisor tries to calm the situation and explains that there is CCTV in operation in the area and asks the customer to leave. The customer becomes violent towards the door supervisor. The door supervisor pushes the customer back at the same time as speaking to him in a calm and measured way, asking him to calm down. The police arrive and the man claims that the door supervisor has assaulted him.

Ask yourself the following questions:

1. Were the door supervisor's actions reasonable?
2. Were the door supervisor's actions necessary?
3. Were the door supervisor's actions in proportion?

If you touch someone in any way without their consent, this could be interpreted as an assault. You must always ask yourself if the action you are taking is justifiable. Is the use of force reasonable, necessary and in proportion? You need to be able to answer yes to all three of these questions for the use of force to be justified.

If the use of force is not justifiable, you could be convicted of assault and end up with a criminal record. If you have a criminal record, your SIA licence will be revoked. If your pub or night club gets a name for itself for having aggressive door staff, the venue will get a bad reputation, which could lead to loss of revenue.

The implications for a venue or employer are that they could be held responsible for excessive use of force or negligence by staff. The use of excessive force can lead to insurances being invalid if physical intervention is used inappropriately.

The use of force may be justified if you are:

- acting to save a life or protect an individual from danger
- acting in self-defence
- preventing a crime
- making a citizen's arrest to lawfully detain an individual
- protecting property.

Any force used must be the minimum required to achieve the objective and must also be appropriate to the situation and the individual on whom the force is being used.

Additionally, you must consider the human rights of the individual, especially if restraining for a period of time prior to the arrival of assistance. They may be in extreme and disproportionate discomfort due to a medical condition or an injury sustained during the physical intervention itself and the resulting restraint.

The law requires that all incidences where physical force has been used and injuries have been sustained are filed under the Reporting of Injuries, Diseases and Dangerous Occurrences Regulations 1995 (RIDDOR).

Regulatory bodies such as the SIA have given permission for companies to give training in physical intervention as part of the skill set required in the security industry. However, they caution that this must be physical intervention that is non-pain compliant. You are not given permission to inflict pain on any member of the public, your colleagues or staff.

Did you know?

RIDDOR is the Reporting of Injuries, Diseases and Dangerous Occurrence Regulations (2005). It states that employers, the self-employed and anyone in control of premises must report specified workplace incidents. Incidents can be reported by various means including on-line, by phone, e-mail and by post.

RIDDOR defines an incident or accident in the use of physical intervention as including acts of non-consensual physical violence. Employers are required to report accidents to the enforcing authority if they result in death, major injury or if they result in a worker being unable to do their duties for more than three days.

For more information go to www.pearsonhotlinks.co.uk

Case study: Unjustified use of force

In 2010, there was a case reported in the Daily Mail that illustrates clearly what can go wrong when the use of force is excessive and unjustified.

A man was seen taking a bottle of perfume from a shop without paying for it. The cost of the perfume was £35. Security officers chased the man and he was caught and brought to the floor. The man put up a struggle and four security officers held the man on the ground. One of the security officers held the suspect around the throat and continued to maintain this hold although the man was clearly in distress and asking the security officers to stop. Members of the public were also asking the security officers to stop.

The security officer only released his grip around the man's neck 10 minutes later once police arrived. By this time, the man had stopped breathing. Police attempted to resuscitate the man but he was dead.

Over to you

1. Do you think that the actions of the security officer were justifiable?

2. Do you think the actions of the security officer were necessary?

3. Was the use of force reasonable?

4. What do you think the legal and professional implications were for the security officer involved?

For a link to this story, please go to www.pearsonhotlinks.co.uk

2. Understand how to reduce the risks of harm when physical intervention skills are used

The use of professional, well-trained staff cannot be over-emphasised when looking at how to reduce risks associated with using physical intervention skills. When trained staff use correct physical intervention techniques, harm or injury can be avoided or minimised. Continual reassessment of procedures, keeping staff trained in current practices and reflecting upon situations and procedures all help to reduce the risk of harm.

The physical intervention techniques do not require force or strength to succeed and, therefore, reduce the risk of injury during the practice of the technique.

It is never acceptable to:

- strike someone

- use restrictive physical intervention which causes pain

- use a restrictive physical intervention as a punishment

- use any procedure which restricts breathing or impacts upon the airways.

Before deciding when to intervene and how much force to use you should also take into account the following individual factors:

- The size, weight, age and overall physical health of the individual are important contributing factors and must be taken into consideration.

- Individuals may be under the influence of alcohol or drugs and become overly aggressive or confused and intimidated in a short space of time. They may also display abnormal levels of strength.

- Individuals may have learning difficulties and/or mental health issues and their behaviour may be based on delusional beliefs. Their actions may be irrational and spontaneous.

Injuries may also occur depending on the location of the physical intervention. Some techniques may not be appropriate in narrow corridors, stairways or on slippery surfaces.

You will probably, at some point in your career, find yourself in a situation where you have no option but to physically intervene. You will have already applied your communication skills to the very best of your ability in an attempt to defuse the situation but a particular individual refuses to cooperate and you are aware that imminent harm will be inflicted on you or someone else if you don't physically intervene.

Before deciding to intervene, you must consider factors such as the size, weight and gender of the individual.

149

Always use the minimum amount of force

When you are in such a situation it is vitally important that you remain:

- **focused** – You will need to focus on the individual and not be distracted by external influences such as other people shouting or trying to intervene themselves. Once you have committed yourself to physically intervening, you will need to act decisively and with efficiency and confidence – and always with the minimum amount of force. If possible, as in escorting a person from the premises, inform the individual of your actions beforehand so that they are aware of what is happening. This will also enable them to have a choice and they may leave of their own accord. If restraint is necessary ensure that you have called for assistance before engaging in action as your colleagues can help restore order and to continue resolving conflict if it is a group situation.

- **in control** – If holding and restraint are necessary it is likely that the individual will try to escape or respond with blows. If this occurs it is essential that you do not meet this aggression with equal violent force. Remember that you will be acting within the law to protect yourself, and those immediately involved, from harm – it is your duty and responsibility not to become personally involved. Remaining in control throughout the procedure will also give the individual you are engaged with the opportunity to stop further violent action and calm down.

- **rational** – Irrational behaviour on the part of the door supervisor will only result in negative consequences and must be avoided. Carefully assessing the situation and making sure of the facts is essential if you are not to make the mistake of wrongful intervention. You will need to gain enough information from those involved to make an informed and rational decision on how to proceed. Remaining calm and factual, confident and efficient will enable the other people involved to see that you are acting considerately and intelligently without bias or favouritism. This may be enough to resolve the issue without the need to physically intervene.

- **professional** – Legal issues surrounding the use of force are often complicated. For this reason it is necessary for you to always be able to justify the force you have used – perhaps even in a court of law where your actions will be brought into question from a professional, ethical and legal perspective. If you are restraining someone or attempting to apprehend a physical aggressor, you should be continually monitoring and re-evaluating the situation. CCTV cameras are often recording actions and confirming that the correct method of restraint was administered.

2.1 The importance of dynamic risk assessment

A **dynamic risk assessment** (see Unit 3 Conflict management for the private security industry, p.122) is a way of constantly assessing a situation as it is occurring. Conducting a dynamic risk assessment enables you to maintain continual awareness of your surroundings and be aware of any potential threats. Awareness and constant vigilance mean that you are always prepared.

Through training and practice, conducting a dynamic risk assessment should become second nature to you. You should continually be asking yourself the following questions:

- Who is around in the venue?

- What is their proximity to you?

- If an incident occurs, what is the best position for you to be in? For example, are you in a tight corner that is impossible to move from, or do you have your back to potential problems?

- Who can you call on for back up and how far away from you are they?

- Where is the nearest exit?

- How can you reduce possible risk? Think about the primary controls that were discussed earlier in the unit.

When conducting a dynamic risk assessment, use the SAFER five point approach:

- Step back – Is physical intervention absolutely necessary? Is there the opportunity to deal with the situation verbally?

- Assess threat – If there is a risk of harm to yourself or others then your actions should be guided so as to minimise or prevent that harm from occurring.

- Find help – Having the support of your colleagues is invaluable in any stressful situation and more so when events are likely to become violent. A trusted colleague can also be a vital witness.

- Evaluate options – You have decided that physical intervention is necessary and you now need to justify your approach legally, ethically and professionally.

- Respond – Whether you are escorting someone from an establishment or restraining a person for a more serious form of behaviour it is essential that you continually re-evaluate the situation as the use of force may need to be reduced or withdrawn altogether.

A dynamic risk assessment also allows you to continuously monitor the situation and assess any changes in risk to all parties involved during and following an intervention. It will also help you to make an informed

Key term

Dynamic risk assessment – a way of constantly assessing a situation as it is occurring.

Activity: Dynamic risk assessment

A customer is lying on the floor. There is an empty bottle next to him. The door supervisor approaches the customer to see if they are OK and moves the bottle out of their way. As the door supervisor moves in closer to check on the customer, a person with a knife steps out of the crowd and injures the door supervisor.

1. What would you do differently in this situation to avoid being injured? Think about things such as calling for back-up and assessing if it is safe to help someone. Think about the need to assess the whole scene rather than just the immediate problem.

2. What do you think would be the safest way of dealing with the situation?

decision about when to de-escalate the use of force or to withdraw it completely.

Remember that you will need to write a detailed report of the incident which will have to show clear justification for your actions.

2.2 Risk factors involved with the use of physical interventions

Before using physical intervention, you must always keep in mind that someone may get injured if it is not used in the correct way.

The use of inappropriate physical intervention can have the potential to cause serious harm or even death. A person could fall and hit their head or suffer an injury from being forced to the ground. Serious harm can be inflicted from the use of strikes or kicks. Interventions that involve sensitive areas of the body, such as the neck, spine or vital organs should always be avoided to reduce the risk factors involved with physical intervention.

One of the biggest concerns when using physical intervention is not to compromise a person's breathing. A restraint that has the possibility of impairing breathing or increases the risk of asphyxia should not be used in any circumstance.

It is important not to restrain people in the **prone** position. The prone position is considered to be dangerous because:

- it restricts the ability of a person to breathe. It can restrict the diaphragm and muscles of the chest wall. This risk is increased if pressure or weight are applied to a person's chest or back.
- there is a reduction in the amount of air that can be ventilated
- the prone position can trigger other risk factors such as asthma or heart conditions.

Other situational factors that increase risk include:

- **environmental hazards** – is the floor uneven or slippery, is there glass on the floor, are you in a tight corner or narrow corridor?
- **staff numbers** – do you have the right amount of staff on hand to help if you need back up?
- **lack of availability of help** – lack of appropriate back up can put door staff in a compromising position and put their safety at risk.
- **threats from others** – are other people likely to get involved to help you or the person you are restraining?
- **increased risk of falls** – are you operating in a confined space, in an area with a slippery floor, or in an elevated area with the risk of falling down stairs?

Key term

Prone – lying face down on the floor.

Activity: Restriction to breathing

Sit up straight in a chair and breathe normally. Now lean forward and touch your toes. Try to breathe in this position.

How did each position feel?

Did you notice a difference in your ability to breathe in each position?

What did you notice about your comfort levels in each position?

Before engaging in physical intervention, you should always ask yourself the following questions:

- Has the person consumed drugs or alcohol?

- What is their overall physical condition?

- What is the person's age?

- Could they be on any medication?

- What is the person's gender? Their size/weight and general physical health?

- Have they recently had a big meal?

- Does the person have any mental health issues?

Holding or restraining the customer should only involve contact with robust areas of the body: arms, legs and torso. It should not involve pressure against a joint, or holding by the neck, hair, fingers or any sexual area.

Why is it important that you only hold or restrain a customer by robust areas of the body?

The scale and nature of the restrictive physical intervention should be proportionate to the behaviour of the customer and the nature of the harm they might cause.

When a restrictive physical intervention is employed, the level of physical restraint should be reduced as soon as the person is calm and it is felt safe to do so.

Restrictive physical intervention should:

- be used at the minimum level for the shortest period of time possible

- be used in the customer's best interests

- be used as a last resort

- avoid contact that might be misinterpreted as sexual

- be accompanied by reassuring speech (as stated in the behavioural guidelines) and never with threats

- always use the upright position with a person kneeling or standing to avoid any respiratory system compromise.

In addition, you should provide medical attention to anyone who is injured or at risk, and inform and update any emergency services who may be attending. It is important to follow up by writing a detailed and factual incident report.

Perhaps the best way of reducing risk is by being alert and vigilant at all times and defusing conflict before it escalates. Being well trained in conflict management and in physical intervention skills will always help to minimise the risk to you and to others when having to use physical intervention.

2.3 Ways of reducing the risk of harm

Once you have completed this unit, you will have the ability to physically intervene using guiding and holding skills and techniques, thereby minimising the risk of harm to yourself and those immediately involved.

If you do have to use physical intervention, you must always try to minimise the risk to yourself and to others. Using the least possible force means that your intervention has the least potential to cause injury and harm. You should always choose the type of physical intervention with the least force and potential to cause injury to achieve your aim.

You should always maintain communication with the person you are restraining to let them know why you are using physical intervention and to reassure them and to calm the situation down. Constant communication will ensure that the subject knows at all times what is happening and why. Although you may be using physical intervention, the tools of conflict management and the importance of communication cannot be understated.

Following the restraint, it is important to communicate with the subject to reassure them, defuse the situation and to check and monitor their wellbeing. Checking on a person after the use of physical intervention ensures that they have not had an adverse reaction to the restraint or action.

It is important for one member of staff to take a lead role. This may be decided as part of a venue's policy. One person taking a lead role will reduce confusion, maintain control and minimise injuries to all parties involved. People taking a support role can work as crowd control, as backup and can communicate with other venue staff as well as external agencies, such as the police or ambulance services.

Once physical intervention has been used, it is important to calm down the situation as soon as it is safe to do so. De-escalation of the situation as early as possible reduces the exposure to risk for all parties involved.

Once the objectives of physical intervention have been achieved it is important to release the subject and not restrain them for longer than necessary. A subject should be monitored after the use of physical intervention and assistance should be given immediately if a person complains or has signs of breathlessness or other adverse reactions.

2.4 Responsibilities immediately following physical interventions

If you have had to use physical intervention in an incident, it is always important to make sure that the customer has not been injured. If a customer is injured or has claimed to be injured then medical attention or examination should always be the first priority.

Always make sure that no member of staff or any other customers at the venue have been injured. If any emergency services have attended, you should make sure that they are updated about circumstances surrounding the incident such as the position, duration and any difficulties experienced during the restraint.

Make sure that the situation is calm and controlled after the use of physical intervention.

After an incident, is a debriefing required? Does the member of staff require support? Being involved in physical intervention can be an unsettling experience and staff and customers may need some form of reassurance. Immediate support and reassurance can help prevent staff becoming traumatised after an event.

Any claims about the validity or the method of intervention should be investigated. Collect CCTV evidence and witness statements and fill out an incident report.

After any event where force has been used, it will be necessary for the door supervisor involved to write a clear and detailed report of the incident. This is a legal requirement and it may well be used in court as a form of evidence. The report may also be used for formal investigations as well as criminal and/or civil proceedings or disciplinary hearings. It is therefore very important that the report is written as soon as possible after the incident, and in the order that the events occurred, so that the details are accurate and can be relied on at a later date.

The overall theme of the report should show that your actions before, during and after the physical intervention were reasonable, lawful and appropriate to the circumstances. It should also explain:

- **how** the incident occurred with details leading up to it
- **what** happened during the incident including conversations and physical actions
- **where** the incident took place (on the dance floor, on the stairs or outside, for example)
- **when** the incident took place including the date, the exact time and how long it lasted
- **why** certain decisions were made (e.g. a request to leave the premises or a decision to use force)
- **who** was involved including the door supervisor, the central individual(s), colleagues, witnesses and personnel from the emergency services.

In more detail, it is important that the report also includes the following:

- details of any injuries sustained by those involved

The importance of having a clear and well documented report of the incident cannot be overstated

- whether first aid was applied, and what first aid was given

- if hospitalisation was involved, which hospital and details of any conversation between the individual and the hospital if known. If the incident results in major injury a RIDDOR report should be sent to the HSE.

The importance of having a clear and well-documented report of the incident cannot be overstated. If details are missing or inaccurate your actions may be misunderstood and you will not be able to defend your actions to the police, your manager or a magistrate in court. Great care should be taken both in compiling the report and preserving it in a safe place. It is evidence that you have acted within the law and with the best interests of all concerned and you may need to prove this.

2.5 Importance of keeping physical intervention knowledge and skills current

Physical intervention knowledge and skills can fade over time, particularly if you have not had to use them for some time. It is important to learn new skills, practise the skills that you already have and ensure that your knowledge is up to date and compliant with current laws. Make sure you learn these skills from a recognised training provider. Legislation and guidance about best practice may change over time. Training and keeping skills current will enable you to keep your level of professionalism at a high standard, reduce risks and re-emphasise that physical intervention is always a last resort and not a first option.

5. Understand good practice to follow after physical intervention

Physical intervention does not end with the incident itself. Staff may need support and reassurance. The use of physical intervention can be a learning experience and something to reflect upon to improve or implement procedures or to look at areas for staff training.

5.1 The importance of accessing help and support following an incident

Physical intervention can be distressing for both parties involved in the incident. It can also be distressing to observe an incident where physical intervention has been necessary. After the use of physical intervention, door supervisors may feel upset, angry, humiliated or may be injured. Immediate support and reassurance can often help staff to move on from an incident quickly and avoid time off from work or even post-traumatic shock.

After a night working on the doors, it is important to relax and have time and space to yourself to wind down. This may help you sleep after a busy and stressful shift but will also help you put any stressful experiences into perspective. Make sure that if an incident does bother you, you seek help from a colleague, friend or family member. Sometimes just talking about what happened and how you felt about it is enough for you to be able to move on from a traumatic experience. Other situations may leave you feeling more upset and traumatised and you may want to seek professional help or counselling.

5.2 The importance of reflecting on and learning from physical intervention situations

Situations in which physical intervention has been necessary are an opportunity to reflect upon what happened. Ask yourself and your team the following questions:

- What went wrong? If physical intervention has been used, something failed at an earlier stage.
- What worked well in the physical intervention?
- What positives can you learn from the experience?
- What did not work?
- What would you do differently next time?
- Do any policies or procedures need to be assessed or new ones introduced?
- Do staff have adequate training?
- Was there enough back up and support?
- Were there any risk factors that you had not taken into consideration?

Reflecting on and learning from situations enables you to share best practice with members of the security team so that situations where physical intervention is used can be reduced or managed more safely. Some things to consider might be:

- surrounding factors contributing to the incident.
- what happened in the hours beforehand (look for triggers or contributing factors).

Case study: Anna, Door Supervisor team leader

I have worked for a large night club venue for many years and I am the team leader for a staff of six door supervisors. At the end of every night at the club, we all sit down and talk about what has happened that night. We discuss incidents and what we did that we felt worked or did not work. We talk about what we might do differently next time. We might discuss specific customers if they pose a particular problem and talk about how we should deal with those individuals in the future. It is also a way of revising and assessing risks. It is a very good way of building good team spirit. We work much better and more closely as a team now that we spend time together after a shift. It also gives us time to relax and chill out after a hectic and perhaps stressful night.

Over to you

1. Have you ever worked in a team situation where you meet regularly and revise your objectives and performance?

2. Do you think a nightly review of what happened would be useful?

3. What else could you do to improve team spirit and help you to work more closely as a team?

Just checking

1. Name the two types of physical intervention.

2. What is the difference between defensive physical skills and physical intervention?

3. Can you name three examples of primary control?

4. Can you suggest alternatives to physical intervention?

5. Why is it important to keep physical intervention skills up to date?

6. Why is it important to keep notes or write a report after an incident?

7. What sort of details should be included in a report?

5.3 Additional factors when reporting and accounting for use of force

When reporting and justifying the use of physical force you should detail the things already mentioned in this unit. Other factors to take into consideration are:

- the customer's behaviour – did their behaviour warrant the use of physical intervention? Was the use of force justified?

- the size and gender of the person restrained

- what staff resources were available

- the presence or absence of witnesses or bystanders

- any potential weapons that could have been used by the subject

- staff responses including the use of physical intervention and the level of force used

- any injuries sustained and first aid and medical support provided

- any admissions to hospital

- any support given to those involved and the follow-up actions required.

Antonio Perez
Door Supervisor

The physical intervention skills that I learnt in this course have given me the confidence to know that I have appropriate and safe intervention skills to draw upon if I ever need them in my job. I always try to defuse a situation before it gets out of hand and put in place strategies to try and prevent any potentially aggressive situations occurring. But sometimes, as a last resort, I do need to use physical intervention when working on the doors. For example, last week at the club where I work, a male had been drinking steadily all night. When he came out to the smoking area he decided to urinate on the wall of the smoking area in front of customers. One door supervisor radioed for some non-urgent back up, while I spoke with the man to let him know that this sort of behaviour was not acceptable.

I asked the customer to clean up the mess with a bucket of water or to leave. The customer let us know that he did not want to clean the mess up and he did not want to leave. My colleague tried to encourage the man to leave by trying to guide and shepherd the man to the exit, explaining why he had to leave the premises. The customer turned violent and tried to grab us. We responded very quickly and grabbed both his arms and put him into a tight figure four lock to escort him out the club, keeping him restrained until he calmed down. Once he calmed down, we again explained to him why his actions were unacceptable and why he now had to leave the club.

Over to you

1. Think about the situation described above. Do you think that this sort of situation would be a common problem that you might face working in private security?

2. How would you feel about having to deal with customers who may be under the influence of alcohol and who may react aggressively to you?

3. What have you covered in this unit that has given you a better understanding of the use of physical intervention in the private security industry?

4. What skills would you need to develop for your goal of working in the private security industry to become a reality?

Glossary

Absconding – leaving, often to avoid prosecution

Access – the means of entry to a premises or building, sometimes called 'ingress'.

Adrenaline – a hormone produced by the adrenal glands which is naturally produced in stressful situations.

Arrest – to take away or deprive a person of their liberty.

Control measure – a preventative measure you put into place to try and make sure that a hazard does not cause a high risk (e.g. a zebra crossing on a busy road, protective boots and a hard hat on a building site, a high-visibility jacket at night).

Defensive physical skills – a range of skills which you can use to protect yourself or another person from assault or injury.

Deterrent – anything that prevents someone from doing something, e.g. a fence, a guard dog, a CCTV camera etc.

Discrimination – treating an individual less favourably than another individual based on his or her age, accent, social status, religion, sex, sexual orientation, race, country of origin, colour, ethnicity or disability

Disorderly conduct – behaviour that is noisy, aggressive, violent or argumentative

Dynamic risk assessment – a way of constantly assessing a situation as it is occurring

Egress – the means of exiting a premises or building, i.e. the way out.

Empathy – understanding and identifying with how someone feels about a situation. It is about putting yourself in their shoes and considering how they feel.

Harassment – any behaviour which is unacceptable to the recipient and creates an atmosphere of intimidation or fear.

Human rights – basic rights and freedoms that belong to every individual.

Human trafficking – the movement of people across borders, usually by force or deception, in order to exploit them for financial gain.

Indictable offence – a serious criminal offence, which must be tried in Crown Court.

Legislation – law which has been created and enacted by a governing body, such as the government.

Necessary – Was the action necessary? Could the person have been persuaded to comply by other means? Was force required to prevent a crime or protect others?

Non-indictable offence – a less serious crime, which is tried in a magistrates' court. Also called a summary offence.

Non-restrictive intervention – the person is free to move of their own accord.

Non-verbal communication – communicating through body language, tone of voice and facial expression.

Physical intervention – the direct or indirect use of force (bodily, physical, mechanical) to limit another person's movement.

Prejudice – a negative opinion about another person based on their outward appearance or social group.

Primary controls – preventative actions to stop incidents in the first place.

Prohibited – banned or not authorised.

Prone – lying face down on the floor.

Proportional – Was the amount of force used appropriate to the situation or was it excessive?

Proxemic zone – spatial boundary determined by your social closeness to another person.

Reasonable – This is about whether it is reasonable to use force in a given situation. Had every other option been tried and exhausted? Could the situation have been left? Was force ultimately the only available option in the circumstances?

Reflection – considering one's own experiences in applying knowledge to practice. It is the process of thinking about what you did, where it went right or wrong and deciding how you will change your behaviour the next time a similar situation occurs.

Restrictive intervention – the person's movement is limited.

Risk – the chance that someone might be harmed by, or as a result of, a hazard.

Secondary control – an early response to incidents as they develop.

Shock – an acute stress reaction usually caused by a traumatic event such as an assault or bereavement.

Unauthorised activities – actions which a company or individual does not permit on their premises. Unauthorised activities are not always illegal.

Victimisation – term used to describe when an employer shows unfair treatment to an individual who has made a complaint against them.

Index